AF541508

Gender Ratio Imbalance

Gender Ratio Imbalance

Creating Societal Instability

Edited by

Meenu Bhatnagar

2012

Icfai Books
The Icfai University Press

Gender Ratio Imbalance – Creating Societal Instability

Editor: Meenu Bhatnagar

First Edition: 2012
Printed in India

Published by

This book is published by IUP.
University Campus, Agartala-Simna Road,
P.O. Kamalghat Sadar, Agartala – 799210, Tripura (West)
E-mail: info@iupindia.org
Website: www.books.iupindia.org

Unless repugnant to the context otherwise, any reference to the words Icfai, Icfai Books, Icfai University Press shall be read and construed as IUP only. This book is not for sale in US and Canada.

ISBN: 978-81-314-2717-0

Contents

Overview

The Book of Songs from traditional Chinese poetery called 'Shi Jing' which was possibly written as early as 1000-700 B.C. offers this advice to parents:

"When a son is born
Let him sleep on the bed,
Clothe him with fine clothes.
And give him jade to play with....

When a daughter is born,
Let her sleep on the ground,
Wrap her in common wrappings,
And give her broken tiles for playthings."

Historically and traditionally, particularly in Asian countries, this opinion seems to have been stuck. Even today, the preference need for a son over the daughter exists and advanced technology of amniocentesis and ultrasound or inexpensive sperm sorting techniques are used by couples to fulfil their desire for a son. Daughters born are either abandoned or given up for adoption to other countries annually. But technology alone cannot be blamed, as there is evidence of female infanticide and foeticide which is still prevalent in rural areas.

Data in 2005 revealed harsh sex ratio imbalance in Asian countries such as India, South Korea, Georgia, Azerbaijan, China and Armenia. The sex determination technology meant to abort female foetuses was largely responsible in skewed sex ratio. Across the world, the female mortality is seen in terms of gender discrimination between male and female child. Better and timely medical facilities and more or better food for boys have played havoc with the survival of a girl child. The gender of the first child is not important for many parents but later it becomes decisive in limiting the size of the family for personal or governmental policy norms. Social and economic factors also play a vital role in a country and a lot depends on the patriarchal or matriarchal system prevalent in a community.

The consequences of gender ratio imbalance are going to affect the stability of a society to a large extent. A deficit in the number of women for marriage would mean large percentage of men would either remain unmarried or would delay their marriages without a solution of finding wives for many generations. Some may remain unmarried for life adding to the woes of already stressed section of society. The role women play as wife, daughter-in-law or mother is, indispensable to the society but what would happen if women want to remain unmarried because of their career aspirations? The survival of the existing family structures is likely to be badly affected in the modern society. In today's one-child norm what if the son decides to remain unmarried. The whole lineage of family would be at risk. Less number of women would lead to violence, trafficking of women, etc.

The book is divided into two sections having 12 articles. The first section has five articles highlighting different perspectives of gender ratio imbalance, societal stability, a girl's right to life, causes and consequences of abnormal sex ratios in human population, missing women and conflicts among young male population and finally the question regarding the national population policy of two-child norm in India. The second section with 7 articles covers the regional and country experiences. The articles examine the preference for male child affecting the populations in Asia, skewed sex ratios in India, interventions to balance sex ratio at birth in rural and urban China and gender preferences in advanced societies of Sweden and Finland.

Section I: Perspectives

The opening article of this section "**Gender Ratio Imbalance: A Threat to Societal Stability**" by *Meenu Bhatnagar* explores the abnormally imbalanced gender ratio which has drawn attention of experts and scholars in both domestic and global situations. Culture-centric and imbalanced sex ratios are an important feature of the past 200 years. The article examines how imbalanced sex ratios could threaten the very stability of the social fabric as long as the society regards girls as economic and social burdens. Further, a number of measures and programmes are being undertaken to check the gender ratio imbalance which is a cause and worry for many tribulations and instability. Several NGOs like CEHAT (Centre for Enquiry Into Health and Allied Themes) and government bodies alike have deemed the ban on Sex Determination Test (SDT) in the Pre-Natal Diagnostic Techniques (Regulation and Prevention of Misuse) Act, 1994, as the most efficient tool to curb the alarming number of female foeticide. Though son preference is ingrained in many Asian cultures including India and China, there are exceptions such as girl preference in Japan. So the article also examines the effect of nuclear families on attitudes to skewed sex ratio.

The issue of girl infanticide or murder of children because they are female is of growing concern in contemporary societies worldwide, as it is a girl's basic right to live. "**A Girl's Right to Live: Female Foeticide and Girl Infanticide**" by *Brigitte Polonovski* and the working group focuses on two main areas: Right to be born (female foeticide) and the right to live (girl infanticide) and discusses the magnitude of the problems in India, China and Caucasus where the discrimination continues beyond birth. Further, the article highlights the causes and consequences which lead to complex female foeticide and reflects diverse political, economic, social, cultural and religious practices, none of which justifies such violation of human rights. Other practices leading to the death of the girl child are 'honour' killings taking place in Afghanistan, Bangladesh, Brazil, Britain, Ecuador, Egypt, France, India, Iran, Iraq, Israel, Jordan, Morocco, Pakistan and the Palestinian territories, Sweden, Switzerland, Turkey and Uganda. Some positive initiatives taken by countries like India, China, South Korea and the Philippines to deal with the foeticide and infanticide of girl children have been very encouraging. It will take generations to change people's mindset but the situation worldwide is so critical that one cannot afford to wait any longer.

In the absence of manipulation, both the sex ratio at birth and the population sex ratio are remarkably constant in human populations. "**Abnormal Sex Ratios in Human Populations: Causes and Consequences**" by *Therese Hesketh* and *Zhu Wei Xing* explores some natural fluctuation in sex ratio which occurs due to wars, natural disasters etc., which is compounded by traditional preference for male offspring leading to huge distortions in the sex ratio in some countries. On an average, just over half of the human population is male but in some regions of the world, the proportion is considerably above this average. The authors examine reasons for this rise and explore its consequences. The wider social and political consequences of these distortions are discussed with particular reference to China, India and South Korea and measures are suggested to help reduce sex-selection which would lead eventually to normalization of the sex ratio. The effect of male surplus will be a major problem in several Asian countries over the next two to three decades though there are indications that the situation may then improve. In South Korea, the sex ratio has already declined and gender preference data from China are also encouraging. The fundamental change in attitudes is starting to happen though the damage for a large number of today's young men and boys has already been done.

The two areas of the world where such imbalances have become significant in the last five decades are: Russia and several Warsaw Pact nations, where there is deficit in adult males and in Asia – particularly in India, China and Pakistan, there is a deficit of women, including female infants and children. "**Missing Women and Bare Branches: Gender Balance and Conflict**" by *Valerie M Hudson* and *Andrea M den Boer* compares the overall sex ratios e.g., Latin America has 98 males per 100 females (using 2000 US Census Bureau figures), but the corresponding figure for Asia is 104.4 males per 100 females. The sheer size of Asia's population: India and China alone comprise approximately 38 percent of the world's population. Thus, the overall sex ratio of the world is 101.3, even though the ratios for the rest of the world (excluding Oceania) range from 93.1 (Europe) to 98.9 (Africa). The Chinese have a special term for rising ratio of adult young men—'bare branches'—of a family tree that will never bear any fruit but maybe be useful as sticks or clubs. Unequal sex ratio in societies will cause increase in crime rates, rate of drug use, smuggling, weapon smuggling, trafficking and prostitution. The society may develop domestic and international markets that kidnap and traffic in women within the country and across the borders. The article has a value addition titled "**Security Concerns and Gender Imbalance**".

The last article in this section "**Gender Inequality: Is the National Population Policy's Objective of Two Child Norm Heading the Correct Way?**" by *SR Patrikar, Col R Bhalwar, Col A Datta* and *DR Basannar* analyzes the transition in terms of family size, sex of first child and sex preference in a rural setting. This descriptive study was carried out to assess the attitude of women towards birth of son, use of contraception methods and sex determination methods in rural village Kasurdi in Pune District. In a country like India which is undergoing demographic transition, sex ratio at birth is a combination of unrecorded female births and excess of female mortality throughout the life course which has a potentially large effect on the overall sex ratio. Preference for son is very strong and has been frequently cited as one of the major obstacles for reducing the national fertility level. Sex of the first child plays an important role in sex preference. While attempting to correct the female sex ratio in our country, there is a need to emphasize programmes and policies that actively improve the status of women and change of attitude towards the female child.

Section II: Experiences

The first article in this section "**How does Son Preference Affect Populations in Asia**" by *Sidney B Westley* and *Minja Kim Choe* examines that the preference for sons has deep social, economic and cultural roots in many East and South Asian societies. During the last 30 years, some societies in Asia began to show an unprecedented preponderance of male births like South Korea, China, Hong Kong, Taiwan, Singapore and some northern and western states of India. It resulted in gender imbalances leading to concerns that shortage of women will lead to difficulties for men in finding wives. The Chinese, Indian and South Korean governments have responded by making prenatal screening for sex identification illegal. China and India have launched campaigns to improve attitudes toward girl children by offering small allowances to parents of girls whereas experience in South Korea indicates that sex-selective abortion peaks and then declines with social and economic modernization. Population projections and survey data suggest that falling fertility and women's reluctance to marry have a larger effect than sex selective abortion on the availability of women in the marriage market.

Prevalent for two thousand years, the ideal sex composition of children to most couples in China was to have one boy and a girl. But the preference for boy has been rising since 1980s in some rural areas thereby raising a serious, common concern which needs to be dealt with urgently. "**Interventions to Balance Sex Ratio at Birth in Rural China**" by *Zheng, Zhenzhen* explores the imbalanced SRB which is quite real but the issue is not that simple as preference for a boy is a traditional and conscious choice of parents. These traditional changes are quite slow compared to social and economic development. The higher SRB are a consequence of combined social problems, caused by multiple factors and need to be resolved in a comprehensive way by the combined efforts of all sectors. Being a complicated social issue, these cannot be solved only by administrative measures. There are mainly two strategies in balancing the SRB—one is to strictly prohibit identification of foetal sex for non-medical purposes and a sex selective abortion while the second is a nationwide campaign on 'Care for Girls'. The article has a value addition titled **"Will Men have Difficulty in Finding a Wife in Urban China?"**.

The phenomenon of sex ratio imbalance has reached alarming proportions in states having no prior history or practice of female infanticide or where forms of discrimination against girls were not strongly evident earlier. **"The Daughter Deficit: Exploring Declining Sex Ratios in India"** by *The International Development Research Center* examines the factors contributing to the male/female imbalance in the selected districts of five Indian states of Madhya Pradesh, Rajasthan, Himachal Pradesh, Punjab and Haryana. The census revealed that the phenomenon of sex ratio imbalance reached alarming proportions in states having no prior history or practice of female infanticide or where forms of discrimination against girls were not strongly evident earlier. The mistreatment of girls spans across the spectrum of Indian regions, economic classes and castes due to complex mix of economic, social and cultural factors. Some of the trends like son preference, disaffection for daughters, family planning for sons, sex selection practices, causes of childhood deaths and these dealing with subsequent consequences are elaborated. The suggestions made include: It will not be enough to counter son-preference; Aversion to daughters has to be squarely confronted through policy measures that increase their economic worth; Support daughters through improved employment opportunities and Recognizing that women's health and education is tied to more than the mothering roles.

Daughters may not be wanted but daughters-in-law are necessary for family well-being and perpetuation. Similarly, not all sons in the family receive equal treatment and those who are left bachelors suffer a lesser fate. "**Dispensable Daughters and Bachelor Sons: Sex Discrimination in North India**" by *Ravinder Kaur* attempts to move beyond currently available explanations of low sex ratios and daughter elimination. Some of the explanations for daughter elimination are: Hypergamy; dowry; women's lower value in wheat farming; seclusion or lack of participation in productive activities; kinship, marriage and descent systems; patrilocality; concentration of proprietary rights in the hands of individual males etc. While families may love their daughters, daughters are the only 'dispensable' members of the family as they represent 'outgoings' as far as the household resources are concerned in contrast to sons. Shortage of women impinges negatively on men who are on the bottom rungs—whether of the family or of the clan because of the transformation occurring in rural areas where effective nuclearsation of family relationships is taking place even within joint family structures. This is resulting in the neglect of obligatory relationships with unmarried siblings and even old parents. With the desire for one son family and zero daughters, the task of redressing the sex ratio imbalance becomes more daunting and consequently our practice of daughter elimination needs to be curtailed.

Highlighting the sex determination technologies which allowed people to retain male and abort female foetuses, the article "**Missing Women and Brides from Faraway: Social Consequences of the Skewed Sex Ratio in India**" by *Ravinder Kaur* examines China report of shortage of brides leading to cross-border marriages, abduction of women and return to traditional system where families adopted infant girls to raise them as future brides for their sons. In India, there was evidence of a return to fraternal polyandry and import of wives from other cultural regions within the country. The social structure and culture intertwined to make sons highly valued while daughters were correspondingly devalued. Families feel a pressing need to invest in the success of sons especially in the absence of social security systems for parents. China practises bride price as marriage payment and India has dowry system (an additional reason for viewing daughters as burdensome), sex ratios in both countries show a devaluation of women's contribution. The growing flexibility in gender roles is yet to be reflected in change in societal perceptions which continue to consider men as the ideal breadwinner and women as eventual contributors only to their in-laws families.

The next article "**Kinship System, Fertility and Son Preference among the Muslims: A Review**" by *Rosina Nasir* and *A K Kalla* illustrates the differences in kinship system between north (by and large patrilineal) and south (by and large matrilineal) of India. It is important to bring about regional disparities in sex preference of the children by the Hindu parents but not by Muslim parents in whom kinship system is traditionally unique. Muslims share their marital system with the Dravidians and inheritance from paternal side with Indo-Aryan system of the north, while Hindus still follow patrilineal inheritance notwithstanding the Hindu Succession Act of 1956. Though dowry and sex selective abortion are the determinants of status among the Hindus, they are generally not practised among the Muslims. Total fertility rates and sex ratios of five Muslim countries (Algeria, Iran, Indonesia, Bangladesh and Turkey) which are in the fertility transition process have been studied. However, the lower education status, economic status and social status (due to patriarchy and religious ideologies) jointly produce circumstances leading to son being seen as the best socio-economic insurance by the Muslim women. The study shows that fertility among the Muslim women is also a consequence of son preference arising out of socio economic compulsions in the absence (due to strict religious prohibition) of sex selective abortions.

The last article in this section "**Understanding Parental Gender Preferences in Advanced Societies: Lessons from Sweden and Finland**" by *Gunnar Anderson, Karsten Hank* and *Andres Vikat* compares childbearing dynamics and possible underlying sex preferences among native majorities and national minorities, namely Finnish born immigrants in Sweden and members of Swedish speaking minority in Finland. In Finland, there is a continuous boy preference among the majority and the Swedish speaking minority as reflected in higher third-birth rates of mothers of two girls than mother of two boys. Similar preferences are found in Finnish-born migrants in Sweden where native born population appears to have developed a girl preference. Hence, there is a clear indication of a preference for having at least one child of each sex. Support is found in interpretation of parental gender preferences which is a longstanding cultural phenomenon, related to the country of childhood socialization rather than the language group.

Section I

Perspectives

1

Gender Ratio Imbalance
A Threat to Societal Stability

Meenu Bhatnagar

The status of gender ratio imbalance has reached alarming proportions at both national and global levels. This article explores the reasons and consequences of this imbalance along with its present status and incidence. The legislative measures and programs undertaken to check gender ratio imbalance have also been highlighted. Although preference for sons has been ingrained for centuries in Asian cultures, a shift in attitudes has been witnessed as detailed in the article.

Introduction

The unusually high gender ratio is drawing attention of experts and scholars the world over and is becoming a serious problem. Gender ratio of newborns refers to the ratio of male newborns to female ones which, with time points to higher than normal figure. Most of the available information refers to the increasing ratio of boys to girls in many of the Asian nations such as China and India, although imbalances exist in other parts of the world as well.

Statistics world over is indicative of a situation detrimental to the survival of a girl child, leading to gender ratio imbalance. Despite all efforts made through governmental policies, regulations, laws, the role of NGOs, the abnormally high gender ratio has drawn attention of experts at both domestic and global levels. Culturally bound, imbalanced sex ratios are an important feature of the past two hundred years and possibly earlier as well.

Gender Imbalance: Reasons and Consequences

The reasons for gender imbalance could be a demographic effect either as a consequence of war, sex-selective abortion, infanticide because of governmental policy (China or India) or large scale migration by male populace unable to take their families with them (Qatar and other gulf countries). Gender imbalance could lead to social unrest in instances of young males unable to find a spouse.

Sex ratio imbalances can also develop from the social process in the society like:

- Migration, both international and domestic
- Wars and armed conflicts in the world
- Incarceration of women in society.

Nuclearization of families in rural or urban areas is adding to the issue of gender preference in a big way. With a girl child in the house, one has to be more alert about her security especially, if both parents are working, couples tend to prefer to have male child only. Sometimes, the career and ambitions being at the forefront, couples delay having children. This often results in other medical complications.

If the global migration keeps increasing, then such imbalances would become more pronounced as new reproductive technologies would allow parents to choose their child's gender. There are varied reasons for imbalance in sex ratios and they pertain to marriage, fertility, human capital development as well as wages[1] and could form a number of complex combinations.

1. Traditional thinking stresses on the importance of males while ignoring the role of females.
2. Such thinking is detrimental to economic growth and social development.

[1] *http://www.honors.ucr.edu/Courses/hnpg041e.htm*

3. Prevalence of incomplete and inadequate social security in rural areas.
4. Backward productivity.
5. Traditional culture of male dominance and gender inequality in society.
6. Another more direct cause is the availability of gender-distinguishing medical techniques.

Measures for Gender Imbalances

If this high ratio among genders is not corrected, then a number of problems will emerge socially.

1. Emergence of 'Marriage Squeeze'[2] where, young men will not find wives.
2. Rise in the number of Bachelors.
3. Rise in sex, outside marriage.
4. Women kidnapping.
5. Organized crime, leading to terrorism.

To control the rise in gender ratio imbalance, a number of measures need to be taken:

1. Strict enforcement of present legislation.
2. Proper execution of laws.
3. Creating awareness through literacy.
4. Recognizing and giving equal rights to women.
5. Supervision of public opinion through awareness campaigns, about the dangers of gender imbalance.
6. Eliminate sex discrimination through technology to arrest its misuse.
7. Put an end to illegal gender determination before birth.
8. Give bonus to the parents of a girl child.
9. Provide social security to the parents of a girl child both in rural and urban areas.

---

[2] *http://english.peopledaily.com.cn/200406/30/eng20040630_148069.html*

Social stability gets adversely affected in societies or cultures that give preference to male babies. This is a primary effect of gender imbalance.

Status of Gender Imbalance

Though demographically much secure, India commonly shares one problem with China, that of gender imbalance. Official data suggests that, on an average, India has 927 women for every 1,000 men. It is much worse in many of the north-western states of India, which has resulted in import of brides from other states.

The long standing practice of preferring sons over daughters has resulted in a gender ratio imbalance in many Asian countries[3]. The introduction of sex-detection ultrasound technology, alongwith the long-term problem of the neglect of girls has resulted in millions of women gone missing from a number of countries.

Sex Ratio Imbalance in India

According to the census data of 2001 the highest and lowest female sex ratios in India at state, union territory and district levels are as follows:

Census Data 2001 – India at a Glance – Sex Ratio		
	Sex ratio (females per thousand males)	
	India	933
	Rural	946
	Urban	900
State with the Highest Female Sex Ratio	Kerala	1,058
State with the Lowest Female Sex Ratio	Haryana	861
UT with the Highest Female Sex Ratio	Pondicherry	1,001
UT with the Lowest Female Sex Ratio	Daman & Diu	710
District with the Highest Female Sex Ratio	Mahe (Pondicherry)	1,147
District with the Lowest Female Sex Ratio	Daman (Daman & Diu)	591
http://www.censusindia.gov.in/Census_Data_2001/India_at_glance/fsex.aspx		

[3] *http://www.thedailystar.net/story.php?nid=42441*

Sex Ratio at Birth

The sex ratio at birth in five states of India *viz.*, Tamil Nadu, Kerala, Uttar Pradesh, Haryana & Punjab for the period from 1999-2001 to 2004-2006 has been graphically shown below:

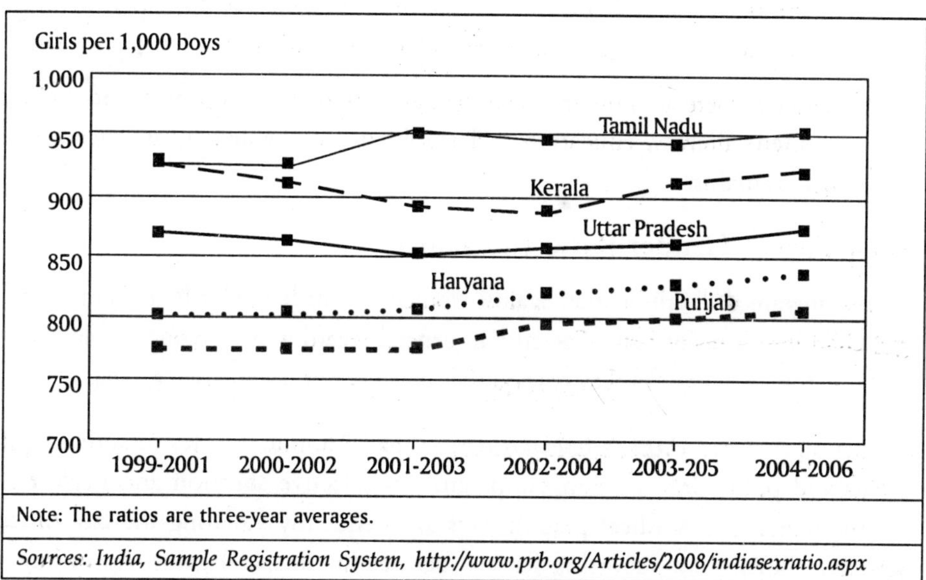

Note: The ratios are three-year averages.

Sources: India, Sample Registration System, http://www.prb.org/Articles/2008/indiasexratio.aspx

A research, conducted in locations across the states in the north and northwest India revealed[4]:

- Ratios of girls to boys till the age of 6 across four out of five states are now lower than in 2001.
- Ratios of girls to boys are declining fast in many of the prosperous urban areas.
- The girls are more likely to be born in the areas with limited access to public health facilities and ultrasound technology, but less likely to survive.
- Low birth rates and higher mortality rates for the second and third daughters through selective abortions and neglect were recorded.
- Modern trend towards smaller families is deepening the aversion to daughters.

---

4 *http://www.seniorwomen.com/ni/niissues.html*

- The banning of laws for prenatal sex detection and sex-selective abortions are being ignored.
- The ultrasound technology is being widely and explicitly being used for sex selection.
- There is tremendous pressure on families to avoid having girls; the use of ultrasound technology is now considered a 'rational' way to plan a family.
- Though there are policies to address girls' rights and improvements towards women's literacy, education and employment, the anxiety to have a male heir remains.

Incidence of Gender Ratio Imbalance

Deeply ingrained discrimination against women has made the birth and survival of a girl child into a major issue. Societies in general regard girls as economic and social burden; consequently, families make an all out effort to avoid having daughters[5].

Action Aid and IDRC's research reveals that, "despite policies to address girls' rights and public information campaigns, sex-selective abortion and neglect are on the increase"[6]. Medical practitioners are frequently violating the ban on sex selective abortion and aborting female foetuses for financial gains. According to recent figures published in *The Lancet*, around 500,000 female foetuses are aborted every year[7]. In poorer communities, daughters die because of neglect, lack of medical care and nutrition. However, the basic social and economic factors that support gender discrimination compel people to make such decisions.

The gender ratio imbalance is based on multiple and complex reasons. One of the main reasons being that, selective foeticide made possible by the modern ultra sound technology. Another possible reason for the gender ratio imbalance could be common Hepatitis B virus. This has been suggested by Nobel Laureate Baruch Blumberg, who indicated that, fathers carrying this virus are more likely to have sons rather than daughters. Thus, this virus could be directly influencing the human species[8].

---

5 *http://www.actionaid.org.uk/index.asp?page_id=101347*

6 Ibid.

7 *http://www.womensenews.org/article.cfm?aid=2672-25k*

8 *http://business.outlookindia.com/inner.aspx?articleid=2089&subcatgid=105&editionid=56&catgid=12*

Gender imbalance could also be caused by differential treatment meted out to daughters and sons at the infant stage, which is a result of a deep-sseated culture bias.

India suffers from gender ratio imbalances and the situation is likely to be getting worse. In addition to the social aspects of gender imbalance, it also has far reaching economic consequences. Skewed sex ratio implies that, in the future in India, there will be disproportionately lesser women to deliver babies, as the number of birth per woman is also declining. Although a fall in population growth may be a welcome phenomenon in the overcrowded countries but if it happens suddenly, then the population would age very quickly, giving rise to the problem of demographic transition.

The PNDT Act

The Pre-Natal Diagnostic Techniques (Regulation and Prevention of Misuse) Act—PC and PNDT Act of 1994 disallows the use of pre-natal diagnostic techniques of sex determination and can be used only for detecting genetic or metabolic disorders, chromosomal abnormalities, certain congenital disorders or sex-linked disorders[9]. Further, the Act adds that, no person conducting the PNDT procedures will communicate to the pregnant women or her relatives the sex of the foetus by any means[10].

The Act was enacted by the Indian Parliament after the 1991 census figures showed the disturbing trends in child sex ratios, which led to the campaigning on the issue by women's and other civil society groups across the country. This Act was upheld by the Mumbai High Court in the case of Mr. & Mrs. Soni vs. Union of India and an NGO—CEHAT (Centre for Enquiry into Health and Allied Themes) 2005. The judge stated that, "The right to life or personal liberty cannot be expanded to mean the right to personal liberty to determine the sex of the child which may come into existence. Right to bring into existence a life in future with a choice to determine the sex of that life in itself is a right"[11].

---

9 *http://www.indiatogether.org/2008/apr/wom-npwwomen.htm*

10 Ibid.

11 Ibid1.

There are many problems in implementing this legislation as by mere enactment of an Act the problems would not vanish. Though the government can override the decisions of a body set up for monitoring the facilities but partial regulation in sex determination and selection have not been able to stop the gender ratio imbalance. From time to time, the government has been amending the PNDT Act 1994, for example, the amendment of February 2003, to give it more teeth[12]. However, the preference for a male child has remained unchanged both in the urban and the rural areas, despite the awareness having been created about perils of gender ratio imbalance.

Shift in Preference – A Ray of Hope

Though son preference is ingrained in many Asian cultures particularly of India and China, a shift in attitude is being witnessed towards girl preference in Japan in the last two decades[13]. Falling birth rates are troubling developed countries around the world. Rising marriage age has led to a further drop in childbearing rate. There is not much research data available on the shifting attitudes of visible daughter preference in Japan and such a lack of interest could be because of its geographic closeness to countries where son preference is very much visible and secondly the country has a higher level of economic development so, Japanese exhibit the least or no preference for a son. Maybe for this reason only it would be interesting to examine the case of Japan which is a low fertility nation. In earlier times, it was generally believed that a daughter would get married and thus be a loss to the family. However, in recent times it is now believed that strong bonding between the daughter and her parents continues even after marriage. On the other hand, a son is more likely to leave the family and move to a far off place of work[14]. Today's advanced reproductive technologies are a tool in the hands of the parents in controlling the gender of their offspring; the daughter preference would get an impetus for ensuring daughters only. In this tendency of having fewer children, it was found that, on the preference for a boy or girl as an only child, majority of the couples opted for a daughter.

---

12 Ibid2.

13 *http://paa2006.princeton.edu/download.aspx?submissionId=60747*

14 *http://web-japan.org/trends98/honbun/ntj980729.html*

It has been observed that ageing generations in Japan are turning to daughters for their old age care and needs, rather than to their sons. On the other hand, it is seen that the sons generally leave the nursing of the aged to their wives. The economic and social development of a country is instrumental in changing the attitudes and preferences from son to daughter. South Korea was a first among the several Asian countries to reverse this trend at birth. But as Japan developed earlier, the change in societal attitudes on this issue also occurred earlier.

Recently, an unexpected preference for girls was found in Portugal, Lithuania, Caribbean and the Czech Republic[15]. This could possibly imply that modernizing societies have fewer economic reasons for preferring sons and more emotional reasons for preferring daughters.

Conclusion

So, to have a stable society with normal sex ratio of male vs. female, it is imperative that, combined efforts of the governments and societies take place. South Korea, Japan and other economically developed nations have managed to set right the gender ratio imbalance by changing their attitudes towards girl child. Women need to be valued and security for their lives should be the main concern of the society. Today, women are adding to the earnings of a household and if they are not there, then the society and country would have to face social and economic loss. Hence, a shift in preferences and attitudes in some countries has brought a ray of hope for bridging the gaps in gender ratio imbalance and bringing stability in the society.

(Meenu Bhatnagar is a Faculty Associate at Icfai Research Centre, Ahmedabad, Gujarat. She can be reached at meenub@ibsindia.org).

References

1. "Imbalance gender ratio a worry of China", by *people's daily online http://english.peopledaily.com.cn/200406/30/eng20040630_148069.html*
2. "Disappearing daughters – sex selection in India", *http://www.actionaid.org.uk/index.asp?page_id=101347-16k*

---

[15] *http://www.wfs.org/futupap00.htm*

3. "Missing Daughter's on Indian Mother's Mind", Kavitha Rao, 16th March, 2006.
4. "Missing Girls – No country for women", Shoma Chatterjee, 29th April, 2008.
5. Ibid.
6. "Daughter Preference in Japan: A Shift in Gender Role Attitudes?" Kane Fuse, December 2007.
7. *http://paa2006.princeton.edu/download.aspx?submissionId=60747*
8. "TYING THE KNOT: The Changing Face of Marriage in Japan", July 28, 1998.
9. "Gender imbalance a threat to stability", Bellinda Kontominas, Medical reporter in Hyderabad, India, October 31, 2007.
10. *http://www.wfs.org/futupap00.htm*

Further Reading

1. Dynamics of Gender Planning and Population: Issues and Challenges – edited by K B Datta. New Delhi, Akansha Pub., 2002.
2. Bare Branches: The Security Implications of Asia's Surplus Male Population by Valier Hudson and Andrea Den Boer (M.I.T. Press), 2005.
3. Violent Land: Single Men and Social Disorder From the Frontier to the Inner City (Harvard University Press, 1996), David T. Courtwright.
4. Sex Ratio Patterns in the Indian Population, Satish Balram Agnihotri, Sage Publications, January 2000.

2

A Girl's Right to Live
Female Foeticide and Girl Infanticide

Brigitte Polonovski

The issue of girl infanticide or murder of children because they are female is of growing concern in contemporary society worldwide as it is a girl's basic right to live. The article focuses on two main areas: right to be born (female foeticide) and the right to live (girl infanticide) and discusses the magnitude of the problems in India, China and Caucasus where the discrimination continues beyond the birth. Further, the article highlights the causes and consequences leading to complex female foeticide and reflects diverse political, economical, social, cultural and religious practices, none of which justifies such violation of human rights. Some positive initiatives taken by countries like India, China, South Korea and the Philippines to deal with the foeticide and infanticide of girl children, have been very encouraging. It will take generations to change people's mindset but the situation worldwide is so critical that one cannot afford to wait any longer.

Source: www.icw-cif.org © Working group on the girl child of the Committee on the Status of Women of the Conference of NGO in Geneva for the session of the UN Commission on the Status of Women 2007. Reprinted with permission of Brigitte Polonovski, chair, on behalf of the working group.

Introduction

The issue of girl infanticide, or the murder of children because they are female, is of growing concern in contemporary society worldwide. This violation of a girl's basic right to live, requires urgent attention and action. The following report, drafted by members of the working group on the girl child (part of the NGO committee on the status of women in Geneva), focuses on two main areas: the right to be born (female foeticide) and the right to live (girl infanticide). The Working Group recognizes these two areas as being of particular importance in the education of the concerned societies. This report also identifies many of the root causes of girl infanticide in the private and public sphere of the society, thus identifying specific actions to be taken.

The publication and presentation of this report is to coincide with the 51st Session of the Commission on the status of women meeting in New York (26 February to 9 March, 2007) focusing on the "Elimination of all forms of discrimination and violence against the girl child". This is hoped that this report will serve as an educational and working tool for civil society, social entrepreneurs, other NGOs and the interfaith community to help them speak out against girl infanticide. Through this report, the Working Group also calls upon governments to get more involved in developing and promoting effective policies to bring an end to the girls' human rights violation of girl infanticide, everywhere in the world.

I. Magnitude

Girl children are undesirable in many regions of the world. In fact, due to the high occurrence of foeticides, infanticides, including newborn neglect and abandonment, the world is currently deprived of over 100 million women. China and India alone are responsible for 80 million missing females. The first warning against this scourge was voiced in 1990 by Amartya Sen—an Indian 1998 Nobel Prize winner in Economy—though since that time the situation has worsened. Economic modernization has exacerbated the phenomenon. Wealth and economic development do not reduce son preference according to Rohini Pande and Anju Malhotra[1]. Isabelle Attané[2] further states that the economic and social liberalization of China has strengthened the traditional social power structure which is

1 Son Preference and Daughter Neglect in India, International Center for Research on Women, 2006, 30th anniversary.
2 Isabelle Attané, L'Asie manque de Femmes, Le Monde Diplomatique, July 2006.

detrimental to women. The use of medical technology for sex-selection and abortion has become a lucrative business. Finally, the girl deficit is more common among educated women and wealthier families.

Female foeticide, the practice of sex-selective abortions, has taken over infanticide, the practice of killing children at birth. Female foeticide is now practiced in different parts of the world but is most prevalent in Southern Asia. This section of the report will consider the magnitude of the problem, the root causes and the consequences of all "missing girls". Finally, we will look at means of enforcing national laws and changing mentalities in order to reassess girls' most basic human right—the right to life.

1. Female Foeticide

The biological norm for birth ratios is about 105 boys born for every 100 girls worldwide. This norm has been drastically altered in some Asian countries such as China and India where the sex-ratio has been skewed since the mid-1980s. In China and India, an average of respectively 117 and 120 boys are born for every 100 girls. The birth ratio has reached 133 boys born for every 100 girls in certain Chinese provinces as well as in New Delhi, Uttar Pradesh, Rajasthan, Bihar, Punjab and Haryana in India. These two countries are joined by Pakistan, Bangladesh, Taiwan, South Korea, Indonesia, Vietnam and the Caucasus (Azerbaidjan, Georgia, Armenia) where female foeticide is also practiced[3]. Given that these countries account for nearly half of the world's population (3 out of the world's 6.5 billion inhabitants), the killing of girls in these countries means fewer wives and mothers for future generations and, as a result, a significant increase in the imbalance of the number of men and women in the world.

India

Female infanticide has been practised in India for thousands of years, but with the increased availability of modern sex determination techniques such as amniocentesis, ultrasound and trans-vaginal probes, sex-selective abortion has become common in most of India's big cities. In 1990, there were 25 million more males than females in India and by 2001, the gender gap had risen to 35 million. Experts now estimate that it may reach 50 million.

---

[3] Isabelle Attané, Une Chine sans Femmes? Perrin, Paris 2005.

Compared to 1991 when only two districts—Salem and Bhind—had an adverse female sex ratio, as many as 51 districts in India now have more male babies born compared to female, according to UNICEF. "In 80 per cent of districts in India, the situation is getting worse"[4].

- According to the UNFPA 2003 statistics, there were 770 girls counted for every 1000 boys in the district of Haryana (one of India's richest states), 814 girls in Ahmedabad (Gujarat), and 845 in South West Delhi.
- According to the Christian Medical Association of India[5] in New Delhi when the third child coming after 2 previous girls is a female foetus, 70% of them are aborted leading to 219 girls for every 1000 boys born. When the first child born is a girl, the birth ratio becomes 558 girls born for every 1000 boys.
- According to the British medical journal *The Lancet* (9 January, 2006), over 10 million female foetuses (1 in every 25) have been aborted in India since 1994. The journal also reports that prenatal sex-selection in India causes the loss of 500,000 girls per year.

China

In 2000, 138 boys were born for every 100 girls in the provinces of Jiangxi and Guangdong, which is 30% above the biological norm.

Caucasus

In 2005, 115 boys were born for every 100 girls in Azerbaijan, 118 and 120 boys for 100 girls in Georgia and Armenia. This points to an alarmingly increasing trend in female foeticide given that in 1995 the biological birth ratios in these countries were recorded as stable.

2. Girl Infanticide

Discrimination does not end with the sex-selective abortion of female foetus. In most cases, it continues beyond birth. Despite the progress made due to government-run programmes for instance in India, the girl child continues to

---

4 UNICEF, 2007 World's Children Report.

5 Christian forum alarmed at female foeticides in Indian capital, Anto Akkara, Ecumenical News International, 18 July, 2005.

lack adequate nutrition, healthcare, education and maternal care. The child mortality data indicates that a larger number of female children do not reach the age of five. And India and China are among the countries where boys far outnumber girls at age five, as reported by UNICEF[6].

Forms of Infanticide

The crude methods of eliminating girl babies after birth include poisoning, throat splitting, starvation, smothering and drowning, which illustrate the insignificance accorded to these young female lives[7].

Cases of female infanticide in Indian North Arrot villages were often reported as natural deaths or still births. Some parents have even succeeded in having false death certificates issued after bribing doctors. The bodies of the infant girls are then burned to destroy any evidence. Further, when evidence surfaced that people were poisoning their girl children, they began to adopt methods such as starving the baby to death[8].

Many other girl children are disposed off, often in garbage dumps. Although some girls are found and revived, most die.

Brutal treatments of mothers and newborn girls have been reported in cases where a daughter is born instead of the desired son[9]. The mother and newly born baby are treated badly because they are viewed as a burden and often receive no medical care.

Eighty to ninety percent of victims of female infanticide are girls of higher birth order (when there are more than two in a family). The girls who survive are likely to suffer neglect as parents often do not hide their contempt for these girls. Most of the killings of these infant girls are committed by senior women in the family.

Each year the number of girls who die is higher than boys. This is an unnatural phenomenon caused, in part, by girl infanticide. A 2001 National Family Health survey in India showed that post neonatal mortality is 13 percent higher for

6 UNICEF, *op. cit.*

7 Gendercide Watch, Female infanticide 2000 p.1-9.

8 Nielsen, Liljestrand, *Hadegaard British Medical Journal* 1997, 24 May, Vol. 314:1521.

9 PHREB, Bangladesh, 2005.

females than for males. Child mortality figures were 43 percent higher for females than for males. Yet, the scientific facts show that genetically girls are considered stronger and more resilient than boys at the time of birth. The abnormal mortality rates, therefore, have to be affected by the tragic reality of girl infanticide, including neglect and abandonment.

Many girls who are granted the right to be born are then denied the right to basic life-sustaining nutrition and health and are instead, neglected by their families and communities. The resulting ill health of the child often leads to death.

Studies have shown that neglect and abandonment during the first few years of life leave a lasting mark on a child's life and can often result in the death of the child[10]. Girl children, in particular, are often victims of deadly neglect and abandonment due to culture, tradition, religious beliefs and social attitudes that continue to make girls vulnerable in the family and the community. In many countries, the girl child endures a low social status that results in fewer rights and benefits than the boy child. In those countries, the issue of adequate food and basic living conditions necessary for the survival of the girl child is of little concern to the members of the communities. These social customs tend to give preference to boys.

Tens of thousands of unwanted baby girls are abandoned in China. Some of the abandoned girls are admitted to the nation's overcrowded orphanages that cannot sufficiently care for the girls[11]. The likelihood of survival beyond one year for newly admitted orphans in China's welfare system was less than 50 percent, although these girls can be subjected to starvation, torture and sexual assault over many years, leading to unnatural deaths[12].

II. Root Causes and Consequences

The root causes leading to female foeticide are complex and reflect diverse political, economical, social, cultural and religious practices, none of which justify such a violation of human rights.

---

10 UNICEF, 2000 State of the world's children.

11 WHO world report on violence, 1999.

12 Death by Default, Human Rights Watch, January 1996.

1. Cultural Factors

India

India has an age old fascination with the boy child. The culture in India is profoundly patriarchal and is a feudal society where women are neither seen nor heard. There is societal pressure for women to have male children and as a result women are often considered failures and tend to feel guilty after giving birth to a girl. Women who are considered to have less value because they did not give their husbands a son are at risk of being beaten and rejected by their husbands. Giving birth to a girl can lead to rejection by in-laws and by the community as a whole. "If you don't kill your girl, you are rejected by the community and/or by your in-laws" acccording to Manjeet Rathee, an English teacher[13].

In the Hindu religion, the son is responsible for lighting his parents' pyre, in order for them to reach Nirvana and having only girls in the family amounts to being condemned to a lower caste in the next world. In Punjab—where the illiteracy rate is close to 70 percent—there are places of worship called "Son temples", exclusively for people who want a male child.

The superstitions are various and some are very detrimental to girls. For example, 'Blessings and curses' of Eunuchs, who travel from village to village to curse mothers who have girls while blessing those with baby boys. Another superstition is that, if the first child is a girl and that girl is killed, the next child will be a boy.

China

Historical Chinese Marriage Customs

"Ever since ancient times, there has been a saying that the three most delightful moments in one's life come with success in the imperial examination, marriage and the birth of a son"[14]. In Confucianism, sons (and particularly the eldest) are responsible for the ancestors' cult.

---

13 *The Sunday Observer,* Ranjit Devraj, 27 July, 2003.

14 Historical Chinese Marriage Customs in Travel China Guide, last updated, 25 December, 2006.

One-Child Policy in China

There are 80 million one-child families[15] and the son preference is particularly prevalent in rural areas, which has led to forced abortion and sterilization. China remains unwilling to give up this policy despite the recognition that it exacerbates the trend to abort female foetuses.

2. Social and Economic Factors

Among the factors which lead to a consideration of females as less valuable, the following are of special importance:

- *Inheritance:* In many regions of rural India there is a strict social taboo on a daughter inheriting land, since if she does so, the land is lost by her father's lineage. If a woman attempted to exercise her legal claim to her share of her parents' immovable property, she would be likely to lose the affection of her brothers together with their sense of obligation to support her in a family emergency or in the event she is widowed without sons. The recent Hindu Succession (Amendment) Act 2005 which deleted the gender discriminatory clause on agricultural land only benefits Hindu women leaving intact the obstacle faced by non-Hindu women.
- Furthermore, women in many rural areas are economically reliant on men who are traditionally the breadwinners, custom which in turn impacts the imbalance in the employment sector.
- Having a boy allows the father to achieve better status in society, whereas, having a baby girl is seen as a curse.
- Not only has the girl child been traditionally considered inferior to boys (she only does domestic chores) but also as a liability—a bride's dowry can financially cripple a poor family. Moreover, the dowry practice can deteriorate into a method of extorsion of wealth from the bride's to the groom's parents, leaving many daughters' parents in debt.
- "Raising a daughter is like watering someone else's field": deep-rooted saying among rural people in China where elderly peasants traditionally can only depend on their sons.

[15] Xinhua, Gender Imbalance in Birth rate, 12 July, 2006.

Nevertheless, in the richest states like Haryana (India), sex-selective abortions are very common and also apply to well-educated women, for whom the girls' deficit is even twice as high as for illiterate women. So, illiteracy and poverty are not the only factors, though we know that much can be achieved through education and improved living conditions. There is evidence that although the dowry was banned in India in 1961 and the caste tradition has been abolished, all these customs are deeply-rooted in the society and still prevail.

In some other areas of Asia, humiliation and even death are often the punishments for a mother who gives birth to a girl, because of the economic hardship and social stigma caused by a female child.

3. Consequences

Over the next 20 years, in parts of China and India, there will be a 12 to 15 percent excess of young men leading to an obvious bride shortage: between 2015 and 2030 there will be 25 million men in China who have no hope of finding a wife[16].

This can give rise to:

- A substantial increase in aggressions and organized crime
- Rape and other forms of violence against women
- Drug and alcohol abuse
- Situation where all men of the family share the same wife
- Women being viewed as commodities: for example kidnapping and trafficking of girls across borders
- Inter-community trafficking, which is something relatively new, such as the "Paros" (women from the outside) phenomenon: women are easily bought just like commodities with a price range between 50 and 900 dollars; the younger the girl, the higher the price. According to UNIFEM, 45,000 "Paros" have been sold in and around Haryana (India) in 2006 alone.

UNICEF[17] has warned that "the alarming decline in the child sex-ratio is likely to result in more girls being married at a younger age, more girls dropping

16 Isabelle Attané, *op. cit.*

17 UNICEF, 2007 *op. cit.*

out of education, increased mortality as a result of early child bearing and an associate increase in acts of violence against girls and women such as rape, abduction, trafficking and forced polyandry".

In a near future, we could see what Amin Maalouf describes in his book *"Le premier siècle* après *Béatrice":*

"Today the social flaw of the male cult could become collective suicide". We would therefore witness the "auto-genocide of the misogynous populations"[18].

III. Positive Initiatives

Results in some countries are encouraging:

1. India

In 1994, India not only banned the misuse of ultrasound and other medical techniques but also condemned sex determination as a criminal offence.

Nevertheless, foeticide is still practiced due to the enormous family and social pressures to produce males. Moreover, they have only bolstered patriarchal values further undermining the status of women:

- Private clinics still openly advertise the services of sex-determination.
- Obstetricians invest in mobile clinics with ultrasound equipment that can be driven into remote rural areas where the preference for male offspring runs high.
- Kits from the US are available that allow women to know the sex of their baby in the comfort of their home.
- Abortion is so lucrative that many doctors do not want to see it curtailed. As a result, 11.2 million illegal abortions are performed each year off-the-record.
- Medical groups also argue that technology used to monitor foetal health—such as ultrasound scans and amniocentesis—cannot be put under such intense scrutiny.

[18] Amin Maalouf, Le Premier siècle après Béatrice, Grasset, Paris, 1992.

- Officials in India say that the phenomenon has become uncontrollable. The reason may also be that "it suits so many people".

In the district of Salem (Tamil Nadu), government schemes suggest that parents should not kill their unwanted girls but abandon them in cradles where 621 babies were left in 2005.[19]

But charities feel this encourages people to throw away babies. In fact, how can such a system that reinforces son preference continue to be promoted?

Many poor families with girls in India were given financial incentives in the name of the infant girls. But like the "cradle baby" scheme, "girl protection schemes" were more the result of political plotting and, therefore, were short-lived even though girl child lives were spared because of those measures[20].

On a more positive note, the Indian State Chief Minister, Bhupinder Singh Hooda declared 2006 the Year of the Girl Child. He introduced an innovative incentive program called "Ladli" or the "adored one", carrying an incentive of Rs.5000 ($100) per year for five years on the birth of a second daughter in a family. If a family has one daughter or only daughters, the parents would be entitled to get old age allowance of Rs.300 ($6) per month after the age of 55. Financial perks are indeed alluring incentives[21].

Where NGOs accompany young mothers and their baby girls from birth to the age of 2 months, giving them food and support, mothers become attached to their daughters and in some places infanticide has decreased up to fifty percent within 10 years[22]. That is why organising "Support groups" with mothers from different backgrounds or ages (mothers in law, young brides, grand-mothers...) to discuss about the issue of the girl child appears to have a very positive impact.

However, the challenge remains:

Decades of policy efforts have not achieved positive change. In fact, the worsening ratios indicate that the situation is deteriorating rather than improving.

---

19 According to Rohini Mohan, CNN IBN 2006.

20 Kirubhakaran, Social Welfare Program, 1993.

21 Anuj Chopra, Gulf News, *Weekend Review,* 31 August, 2006.

22 Documentary broadcast on TV Channel ARTE: "La malédiction de naître fille" *THEMA,* 24 October, 2006.

Today, the focus of most Indian government policies related to son preference has been on reducing sex-selective abortions, but with little or no result.

UNICEF[23] notes that while the pre-natal diagnostic testing legislation has been passed in India, the enforcement is lagging with only one conviction to date.

Female foeticide can be considered as a mass crime facilitated by the medical community. Local initiatives by NGOs are to be encouraged as they do wonderful work on the ground and have the ability to save many lives.

2. China

The program "Care for Girls" was launched by the State Population and Family Planning Commission in 2003 in 24 pilot countries. This program provides social benefits, including cash payments, to families with only girls in order to enhance the status of girls and women. Through such measures, some Chinese families have come out of poverty as they are entitled to accommodation and pensions when they get old. These families begin to feel more confident in the future and become less afraid of having girls[24].

Kong Dehong, a 77th generation descendant of Confucius has recently declared: "In the feudal society, men were superior to women. I guess that is why, women were not qualified to be included in the family tree. Our women are equal now. We have to adapt to the times". So, there has been a change and we hope that this big step will have an effect on reducing the discrimination of the girl child[25].

3. Other Countries

South Korea

Government policies in South Korea have also succeeded in reversing the trend quite rapidly. From the mid-nineties, the government took measures to reverse this trend with positive results so that the girl vs. boy ratio is almost back to normal. There is evidence here that political will is of prime importance in achieving desired results. Enforcing laws and implementing policies are possible as long as all participants pursue the same objective[26].

23 UNICEF: *op. cit.*

24 China promotes girls to avoid glut of bachelors, *China Daily*, 08 August, 2006.

25 Jane Macartney, *The Times UK*, 28 September, 2006.

26 Isabelle Attané, *op. cit.*

The Philippines

In the Philippines, an anti-child abuse, discrimination and exploitation division was established[27]. A children's training workshop on the girl child was also held which celebrated a week for the protection and fair gender treatment of the girl child.

Conclusion

The magnitude of the phenomena of female foeticide and girl infanticide in India, China and other parts of Asia has reached a critical level creating a worldwide demographic imbalance with, in turn, drastic economic and social consequences. Over 100 million women are now missing in Asia which will result in a 12 to 15 percent excess of young men in the next twenty years.

This report has argued that female foeticides or sex selective abortions, promoted by modern medical techniques, have dramatically increased in the last ten years thus exacerbating the killing of girls. Yet, nothing can justify these killings.

As Swami Agnivesh, religious leader and social activist, said last year when talking about foeticides: "There's no other form of violence that's more painful, more abhorrent, more shameful".

Female foeticide not only denies the girl child her most basic human right—the right to be born—but, it also turns women into silent victims. Scientific evidence has shown that mothers who have been put under pressure to kill their baby girls remain deeply hurt and injured for the rest of their lives as they cannot forget their own offspring.

This report has mainly focused on two areas on the killing of girls but other practices leading to the death of the girl child need to be mentioned:

"Honour" killing, usually defined as an act of murder in which a woman or a girl is killed for her actual or perceived immoral behaviour, tends to affect a large number of countries due to increasing migration. "Honour" killings are either decided and performed by the parents or relatives of the woman or girl or by the

---

27 Reported by Canadian International Development Agency (CIDA) Project, 2004.

state as in the case of stoning. Such killings have been reported *inter alia* in Afghanistan, Bangladesh, Brazil, Britain, Ecuador, Egypt, France, India, Iran, Iraq, Israel, Italy, Jordan, Morocco, Pakistan, the Palestinian Territories, Sweden, Switzerland, Turkey and Uganda.

Sexual abuse of girl children is also often fatal and takes many forms including rape and sexual exploitation including the phenomenon of snuff movies[28] made possible through the misuse of new mediatechnologies. During war time, rape is used as a weapon of war and as a way of durably humiliating the enemy, thus exacerbating violence. Contamination by HIV-AIDS of young "virgins" as a way of purification of the man is also leading to the death of very young girls.

Additionally, female genital mutilation and early marriage with its consequences of exceedingly young childbearing are practices which result in medical complications and often lead to the early death of the girl child.

It will take generations to change people's mindset but the situation worldwide is so dramatic that we cannot afford to wait any longer. It is imperative that the International community calls on the governments and all actors responsible for this human and demographic tragedy to enact laws and take urgent measures to fight these violence and discrimination which, by denying the first basic right of all—the right to life—denies all other human rights.

Statement to CSW 51

Working Group on the Girl Child of the NGO Committee on the Status of Women in Geneva

Written statement to the 51st Session of the Commission on the Status of Women – 26 February-9 March 2007.

Submitted and endorsed by the following NGOs:

Association Country Women of the World

---

[28] Snuff movies are short films, generally of bad quality, showing a (supposedly) real murder, often preceded by pornography including women and child rape.

European Federation of Women Active in the Home—Fédération Européenne des Femmes Actives au Foyer

Federation of American Women's Clubs Overseas

Femmes Africa Solidarité

Institute for Family Policy

Inter-African Committee on Traditional Practices

International Association of Gerontology and Geriatrics

International Council of Jewish Women

International Council of Women—Conseil International des Femmes

International Federation of University Women

International Inner Wheel

Pan Pacific and South East Asia Women's Association International

Women's International League for Peace and Freedom

Women's International Zionist Organization

Women's World Summit Foundation

World Movement of Mothers—Mouvement Mondial des Mères

World Union of Catholic Women's Organization

Worldwide Organization for Women

We, the above named Non Governmental Organizations in consultative status with ECOSOC, through this statement and our report on girl infanticide and female foeticide that will be presented and distributed during the CSW in its 51st session, re-affirm and call attention to the inherent dignity and the equal and inalienable rights of the girl child. Despite the legal human rights framework and namely the Convention on the Rights of the Child (CRC), we are deeply concerned with the phenomena of girl infanticide and female foeticide, which deny the girl child the most basic human right, the right to be born. Not only has the status of the girl child not improved but in many regions of the world, it has worsened and its future is threatened.

Girl infanticide, which consists of killing a baby girl at or very soon after birth is a traditional practice most common in India and China, but also spreading to other parts of Asia.

Female foeticide is a modern version of infanticide which consists of killing a female foetus *via* sex-selective abortions. Female foeticide, which has rapidly increased over the last decade, is even more perverse than girl infanticide in that modern technology has made it easier, more silent and an industry has developed to promote it.

Both these practices are based on the traditional belief that a girl is less valuable than a boy, and therefore, is not worth living. Mainly, due to cultural, religious or social factors and practices, such as dowry requirements and inheritance laws, having a girl child is still considered a burden or a failure in many countries. There is no rational explanation for this phenomenon, given the knowledge that sex-selective abortions are even more common in wealthier and educated families.

The magnitude of this human rights violation is building to a worrisome demographic imbalance with economical and social consequences worldwide:

- Killing of girls in the most populated countries means fewer wives and mothers and in turn, fewer girls and mothers for future generations resulting into a greater imbalance in the number of men and women in the world. Over 100 million women are missing, which will result in a 12 to 15 per cent excess of young men in the next twenty years and therefore a bride shortage. For example, between 2015 and 2030, 25 million Chinese will have no hope of finding a wife[29].
- Trafficking of girls and women across borders and within communities is developing at an alarmingly high speed. This only enhances the traditional power structure detrimental to women: becoming seen as a commodity and therefore holding less value. The "paros" phenomenon or the import of "women from the outside" sadly illustrates this situation as girls are easily bought—and the younger the girl, the higher the price.

---

29 Isabelle Attané, Une Chine sans Femmes? Perrin, Paris 2005 and L'Asie manque de Femmes, article from Le Monde Diplomatique, July 2006.

- Forced marriages are increasing dramatically, in some cases, forcing young women into marrying and belonging to several men at the same time.

The phenomena of girl infanticide and female foeticide are alarming and this is the reason why we are calling upon the UN Commission on the Status of Women, in its 51st session focusing on the elimination of all forms of discrimination and violence against the girl child to:

- Reaffirm the equal dignity of men and women and especially the right to be born.

We also call upon the UN CSW to request political commitment from governments to:

- Strengthen and implement laws against girl infanticide;
- Amend laws that create and support the conditions where women are seen as a burden, such as inheritance laws and dowry requirements;
- Create an environment favourable to girls, for example by giving allowances to families who welcome girls;
- Provide education on gender equality;
  - Support good local initiatives from NGOs which support families with girl children from pregnancy onwards.

Madame Chair, nothing can justify the mass-killing, torture, ill-treatment or sale of girls. We expect that at this UN CSW, a recommendation will be adopted to address this deplorable situation.

Reference to Major Treaties and Other Documents

Convention on the Rights of the Child (1989), and its optional protocols (2000).

Convention on the Elimination of all Forms of Discrimination Against Women (CEDAW) (1979), and its optional protocol (1999).

International Covenant on Economic, Social and Cultural Rights (1966).

International Covenant on Civil and Political Rights (1966).

Beijing Declaration and Platform for Action (1995).

"Beijing +5" Political Declaration and Outcome Document (2000) and all follow up, including the CSW Special Session "Beijing+10" (2005).

– Millenium Development Goals (MDGs) (2000).
– Universal Declaration of Human Rights (1948).
– Charter of the United Nations (1947).

Summary

Principal causes for female foeticide and girl infanticide

- Traditions:
  - Social pressure stronger than law
  - Girls considered as a useless economic burden
  - Misunderstanding of the importance of the committed crime
  - Non respect of women's rights
  - Exclusion of women from their societies if traditions are not followed
  - Superstition, religious beliefs.
- Illiteracy:
  - Ignorance of the human body and the way it functions
  - Ignorance of the laws in force
  - Poverty.

Principal consequences of female foeticide and girl infanticide

- For women:
  - High risk of death
  - High risk of disease/malformation
  - Mental traumatism
  - For society.

Demographic imbalance (e.g., villages of bachelors in India, lack of young women in age of marriage in China, etc...); this creating, among other things, violence, alcoholism, theft, depression, drugs and rape.

Actions/Recommendations

Non Governmental Organisations (NGOs) should:

- Make sure that:
  - National governments implement international treaties;
  - Local governments are aware of women's and girls' rights;
  - Co-operation and information-sharing within the NGO community are facilitated.
- Draw the attention of professional bodies (doctors, lawyers, social workers, etc.,) to women and girls' human rights and make them aware of equal rights between men and women.
- Urge heads of different religious communities in the world to contribute toward making traditions evolve according to the Beijing Platform for Action.
- Support village (community) education committees with the help of specially trained educators in girls' rights.
- Promote programs including "gender equality" for teachers training children and adults.
- Educate men/women, boys/girls to have a better understanding of the specific needs or situations of women and girls (health, nutrition, security, empowerment...).
- Reinforce girls'educational skills to empower them to become more self-reliant and thus less vulnerable to conditions which can lead to death.
- Better support mothers through the establishment of feeding programs so girls can flourish.
- Urge governments to:
  - Review and implement laws concerning sanctions for infanticide.
  - Foresee special allowances in the case of female birth.

Without girls... no society

3

Abnormal Sex Ratios in Human Populations: Causes and Consequences

Therese Hesketh and Zhu Wei Xing

In the absence of manipulation, both the sex ratio at birth and the population sex ratio are remarkably constant in human populations. Small alterations do occur naturally; for example, a small excess of male births has been reported to occur during and after war. The tradition of son preference, however, has distorted these natural sex ratios in large parts of Asia and North Africa. This son preference is manifest in sex-selective abortion and in discrimination in taking care of girls, both of which lead to higher female mortality. Differential gender mortality has been a documented problem for decades and led to reports in the early 1990s of 100 million "missing women" across the developing world. Since that time, improved health care and conditions for women have resulted in reduction in female mortality, but, these advances have now been offset by a huge increase in the use of sex-selective abortion, which became available in the mid-1980s. Largely as a result of this practice, there are now an estimated

---

Source: www.pnas.org, Proceedings of the National Academy of Sciences of the United States of America (PNAS), September 5, 2006, Vol. 103, No. 36, 13271-13275.

80 million missing females in India and China alone. The large cohorts of "surplus" males now reaching adulthood are predominantly of low socio-economic class, and concerns have been expressed that their lack of marriageability and consequent marginalization in the society, may lead to antisocial behaviour and violence, threatening societal stability and security. Measures to reduce sex selection must include strict enforcement of existing legislation, the ensuring of equal rights for women and public awareness campaigns about the dangers of gender imbalance.

Just over half of the human population is male. In 2004, males accounted for 50.4% of the global total (1), but in some regions of the world, the proportion is considerably above this average. Here, we examine the reasons for this rise and explore its consequences. We first explain how some natural fluctuation in sex ratio occurs in human populations, and we illustrate this with the example of the effects of war. We then demonstrate, how the tradition of preference for male offspring has led to huge distortions in the sex ratio in some countries. The wider social and political consequences of these distortions are discussed, with particular reference to China, India and South Korea. Finally, we suggest measures that will help to reduce sex selection and lead eventually, to normalization of the sex ratio.

The Sex Ratio at Birth and the Population Sex Ratio

These two terms need to be clearly differentiated. The "sex ratio at birth" is defined as the number of male live births for every 100 female births. Accurate figures for sex ratio at birth are difficult to obtain in many populations because of inadequacy of vital statistics registration (2). In particular, births occurring at home and births of unwanted or abandoned infants often go unrecorded. In China, the One Child Policy presents specific challenges to accurate data collection because, there may be collusion between parents and authorities to hide births that are not approved within the Policy (3).

In the absence of manipulation, the sex ratio at birth is remarkably consistent across human populations, with 105-107 male births for every 100 female births.

This slight excess of male births was first documented in 1710 by John Graunt and colleagues for the population of London (4) and many studies of human populations have confirmed their finding. A key study of births for the period 1962 to 1980 in 24 countries in Europe showed a sex ratio of 105-107, with a median of 105.9 (5). The latter figure is widely used as the baseline for calculating deviations in the sex ratio.

Over 30 demographic and environmental factors have been studied for their effects on the sex ratio at birth, including family size, parental age, parental occupation, birth order, race, coital rate, hormonal treatments, exposure to environmental toxins, stress, several diseases and war (6-9). The finding of a small but significant increase in male births during and after war has been documented in Europe and the US, in both the First and Second World Wars (10-12) and in the US for the Korean and Vietnam Wars (13). However, studies of the Balkan Wars (14) and of the Iran-Iraq war (15) did not reproduce these findings. Proposed biological explanations for the observed increase in sex ratio during war include stress to adult males, affecting the viability of XY-bearing vs. XX-bearing sperm; changes in the age structure of the population; and higher frequency of intercourse, leading to conception earlier in the menstrual cycle, all of which have been associated with increased sex ratios in other studies (16-18). Alternatively, evolutionary explanations argue that the increase represents an adaptive equilibrium after the decimation of males during war (13), although critics argue that the increase does not last long enough to compensate for wartime casualties (19, 20). The cause of this alteration in sex ratio at birth during war remains a curiosity.

The "population sex ratio" refers to the total number of males for every 100 females in the population. Figures for this ratio are generally taken from census data and are regarded as more reliable than figures for sex ratio at birth. The population sex ratio depends on three factors: the sex ratio at birth, differential mortality rates between the sexes at different ages, and losses and gains through migration (5). Although sex ratio at birth favours males, differential gender mortality favours females (8). Females have greater resistance to disease throughout life and greater overall longevity, so in circumstances where they have the same nutrition and health care as males, females have lower mortalities across all age groups (21). The situation for men is compounded by their greater tendency to engage in risk behaviours and violence, thus increasing their risk of premature mortality (22). By using Western life tables, drawn from gender-neutral countries, the population sex ratio is calculated at between 97.9 and 100.3 (5).

The Problem of Son Preference

In many countries, however, the sex ratio deviates from these norms because of the tradition of son preference. Son preference is most prevalent in an arc of countries from East Asia through South Asia to the Middle East and North Africa (23). Sons are preferred because (*i*) they have a higher wage-earning capacity, especially in agrarian economies (24) (*ii*) they continue the family line and (*iii*) they are generally recipients of inheritance (25, 26). Girls are often considered an economic burden because of the dowry system; after marriage, they typically become members of the husband's family, ceasing to have responsibility for their parents in illness and old age (27).

Son preference is manifest prenatally, through sex-determination and sex-selective abortion and postnatally through neglect and abandonment of female children, which leads to higher female mortality (28). Since pre-natal sex determination became available in the mid-1980s it has made a major contribution to imbalances in the sex ratio seen in many Asian countries (29). However, it is the combination of sex-selective technology and a small-family culture that has caused the highest sex ratios (29, 30). When large family size is the norm and access to contraception is limited, son preference has little influence on sex ratio because, couples continue bearing children, largely irrespective of the gender of the children (31). Female infanticide, abandonment of newborn girls and neglect of daughters have been used in such societies to increase the male-to-female ratio in families, especially in situations where poverty has limited the number of desired children (25). When the family size norm is moderate and only contraceptive methods are available, couples may consider the sex distribution of their existing children and decide whether or not to use family planning, weighing the need for a son against their desired family size (31). However, when fertility rates are low, by choice or coercion, female births must be prevented to allow for the desired number of sons within the family size norm.

Postnatally, discrimination against daughters leads to neglect of their health care or nutrition, resulting in higher female mortality. A number of studies have shown that unequal access to health care is the most important factor (32, 33). This is especially the case in societies where health care costs have to be borne by the family (34-36). In 1990, Sen (21) estimated that, differential female mortality had resulted in ≈100 million "missing females" across the developing world. Klasen (30) and Coale (5) arrived at the figures of ≈93 million and ≈90 million, respectively, with the highest percentages of missing females occurring in the Indian subcontinent: Pakistan (11% of all missing females), India (9.4%) and Bangladesh (8.9%).

Since the mid-1980s, female disadvantage in mortality has declined substantially, only to be replaced by a different type of disadvantage: sex-selective abortion (28). The combination of widespread access to noninvasive sex-selective technology (ultrasound) and the advent of the small-family culture happened to coincide in some Asian countries in the mid-1980s and has led to a greatly increased sex ratio at birth (25, 31, 37). Realization of the potentially disastrous effects of this distortion has led many Asian governments, including those of India and China, to outlaw prenatal sex-determination and sex-selective abortion, yet, these techniques are still being carried out on a large scale, with virtual impunity (38, 39).

The Impact of Son Preference on Sex Ratio

The impact of son preference on the population sex ratio can be seen in census data for 2001. Asia is the only continent with a sex ratio >100, at 104; North America stands at 96.8 and Africa at 99.8 (40). Table 1 shows estimates for numbers of missing females for Afghanistan, Bangladesh, China, India, South Korea, Pakistan, Taiwan, and Iran. Across these countries, an estimated 67-92 million females were missing in 2001. Three of these countries are of particular interest: South Korea because it has succeeded in reducing the sex ratio very substantially, India because of its marked regional differences in sex ratio and China with its unique One Child Policy.

Table 1: Numbers of Missing Females for Selected Asian Countries, 2001

Country	Calculated No. of Missing females, in millions*
Afghanistan	0.5-1
Bangladesh	1.8-3.7
China	34-41
India	27-39
South Korea	0.2-0.3
Pakistan	2.6-4.9
Taiwan	0.4-0.6
Iran	0.8-1.2
**Adapted from references 28 and 45.*	

South Korea was the first country to report very high sex ratios at birth because, the widespread use of sex-selective technology in South Korea preceded that of other Asian countries. High-quality health care and accurate vital information registration have meant that differential gender mortality and under-reporting have not contributed to abnormal sex ratios (29). The sex ratios began to rise in the mid-1980s in cities, and ultrasound was already widely available even in rural areas by 1990. The large city of Taegu reported a sex ratio of 122-130 in 1990, although it had been normal in 1980 (29). The sex ratio across birth order is well-illustrated by data for South Korea, during the highest sex ratio years of the late 1980s and the early 1990s (see Table 2). These data show that South Koreans select sex even in their first pregnancy because, there is a traditional preference for the first-born to be male (31) and that the tendency to select sex rises for third and fourth births as parents try to ensure that they produce a son. In 1992, the sex ratio for fourth births in South Korea was an astounding 229, whereas, the overall ratio was 114 (31). From the mid-1990s, the government launched a public awareness campaign warning of the dangers of such distortion. Laws forbidding sex-selection technology were more strictly enforced and there was a widespread and influential media campaign focusing on the anticipated shortage of brides (31, 41). Together, these actions led to a decline in the sex ratio from 116 in 1998 to 110 in 2004 (1).

In India, because of incomplete birth registration, sex ratios in young children are used as a proxy measure. The sex ratio in children under age 6 rose from 106 in 1991 to 108 in 2001 (42), showing that, improved health care and general conditions for females have been offset by increased recourse to sex-selective abortion (2). However, distinct geographical differences in sex ratio have appeared across the country; several states in the north and west have very high population sex ratios. For example, in the Punjab, Delhi and Gujarat, ratios are between 114 and 126, but in the south and east, several states such as Kerala and Andhra Pradesh have sex ratios of ≈105 (42). The underlying reasons for this divide are unclear and are not explained by any of the more obvious factors, such as income level, availability of medical resources, variations in economic growth, religion, or differences in female education (2). What is clear is that, where sex selection occurs it is strongly influenced by the gender of the preceding child; for second births with one preceding girl the ratio is 132, and for third births with two previous girls the ratio is 139. In cases where the previous child was a boy, sex ratios are normal (39). In contrast, in Pakistan and Bangladesh sex-selective abortion is much less acceptable and available. In both of these countries, improved health care and conditions for women have led to lower sex ratios (28). The proportion of missing women in Pakistan and Bangladesh has been estimated to have declined from 11% and 8.9% respectively, in 1981 to 7.8% and 6.9% 10 years later (30). Data for Pakistan for 1998 showed further improvement to 6.3% (28).

Table 2: Sex Ratios at Birth, by Birth Order – China and South Korea

Year	Total	Birth Order				
		1	2	3	4	5+
China						
1981	108	105	107	113	115	109
1989	114	105	120	125	133	130
2001	116	106	124	128	131	
Urban	116	113	130	119	119	
Rural	115	105	123	129	132	
South Korea						
1980	104	106	104	103	99	
1989	112	104	113	185	209	
1992	114	106	113	196	229	
2001	108	106	108	120	128	

Adapted from references 27 and 61.

In China alone approximately 1 million excess male births are reported every year (41). Because of the One Child Policy introduced in 1979, China is unique in having a compulsory low-fertility culture, and this is combined with a strong tradition of son preference. In China, there has been a steady increase in the reported sex ratio at birth from 106 in 1979 to 111 in 1990 and to 117 in 2001 (43), increasing to as high as 130 in some rural counties (44). The sex ratio by birth order is particularly interesting in China because of the urban/rural differences in implementation of the One Child Policy (see Table 2). In urban China, only one child is allowed, so, some urban Chinese make the choice to select sex with their first pregnancy. In most rural areas, if the first child is a girl the couple are allowed a second pregnancy. So, if the second (or subsequent) pregnancy is female, either the foetus is aborted or the newborn female child may be abandoned or sometimes simply not registered, allowing the couple to go on to have another child (38).

The Consequences of High Sex Ratios

Because prenatal sex determination only began to be available in about 1985, the resulting large cohorts of "surplus" young men are now only reaching reproductive age. Because of this, the consequences of this male surplus are largely speculative. Many of the outcomes that we have described as consequences, for example, increased levels of violence, are likely to be multifactorial in causation and therefore, impossible to attribute simply to gender imbalance. However, it is not in dispute that over the next 20 years in large parts of Asia there will be an excess of males. In parts of China and India, there will be a 12-15% excess of young men. These men will remain single and will be unable to have families, in societies where marriage is regarded as virtually universal and social status and acceptance depend, in large part, on being married and creating a new family (45).

An additional problem is that, many of these men are rural peasants of low socio-economic class and with limited education (46). When there is a shortage of women in the marriage market, the women can "marry up", inevitably leaving the least desirable men with no marriage prospects (47). For example, in China 94% of all unmarried people age 28-49 are male and 97% of them have not completed high school (48). So, in many communities today, there are growing numbers of young men in the lower echelons of the society, who are marginalized because of lack of family prospects and who have little outlet for sexual energy. A number of commentators predict that this situation will lead to increased levels of antisocial behaviour and violence and will ultimately present a threat to the stability and security of the society (31, 45-49).

There is some empirical evidence to fear such a scenario. Gender is a well-established individual-level correlate of crime and especially violent crime (50). It is a consistent finding across cultures that an overwhelming percentage of violent crime is perpetrated by young, un-married, low-status males (50-52). In India, a study carried out between 1980 and 1982 showed a strong correlation between homicide rates in individual states across the country and the sex ratio in those states, after controlling for potential confounders such as urbanization and poverty (53). The authors concluded that there was a clear link between sex ratio and violence as a whole, not just violence against women as might be assumed when there is a shortage of females. These analyses were repeated by Hudson and Den Boer (46), who showed that the relationship between sex ratio and murder rates at the level of the Indian state persisted through the late 1990s. In China, young male migrant workers are thought to be responsible for a disproportionate amount of urban crime, especially violent crime. It is reported that migrants account for 50% of all criminal cases in the major receiving cities for migrants, with some cities reporting up to 80% (54).

There is also evidence that, when single young men congregate, the potential for more organized aggression is likely to increase substantially (45, 53). Hudson and Den Boer, in their provocative writings on this subject (45, 46), go further, predicting that these men are likely to be attracted to military or military-type organizations, with the potential to be a trigger for large-scale domestic and international violence. With 40% of the world's population living in China and India, the authors argue that the sex imbalance could impact regional and global security, especially because the surrounding countries of Pakistan, Taiwan, Nepal and Bangladesh also have high sex ratios.

A number of other consequences of an excess of men have been described, but there is very little evidence for causation. It is intuitive that if sexual needs are to be met this will lead to a large expansion of the sex industry, including its more unacceptable practices such as coercion and trafficking. The sex industry has expanded in both India and China in the last decade (55, 56); however, there are a number of reasons for this expansion and the part played by a high sex ratio is impossible to isolate without specific research addressing this question. Indeed, in China the highest numbers of sex workers are in areas where the sex ratio is least distorted, for example, in the border areas of Yunnan Province (57). The recent rise in numbers of sex workers in China has been attributed more to greater mobility, increased socio-economic inequality, and a relaxation in sexual attitudes, than to an increase in the sex ratio (57, 58).

There is much anecdotal evidence regarding increases in trafficking of women, both for the sex industry and marriage, in both India and China (59, 60), although it is impossible to say whether gender imbalance is a contributory factor in this rise. Reports would suggest that trafficking is more common in parts of Africa and Eastern Europe where the sex ratio is normal (61). It has also been suggested that a shortage of women may lead to a rise in homosexual behavior (31), not implying that the shortage of women will produce homosexuals, but rather that an increasing tolerance toward homosexuality, together with the surplus of males, may lead to large numbers of covert homosexuals openly expressing their sexuality.

The latter could be viewed as a positive outcome and there are others. First, access to prenatal sex determination results in an increase in the proportion of wanted births, leading to less discrimination against girl children and lower female mortality. India, South Korea, China, Pakistan and Bangladesh have all reported reductions in differential mortality in the last decade (2, 28). Second, gender imbalance will lead to a reduction in birth rate, which may be particularly beneficial in countries trying to control population growth (47). Third, as the number of women in a society decreases, so their social status should increase and they should benefit from their enhanced value (48). Ultimately, this may lead to more balanced sex ratios because couples will choose to have girls. However, it has also been argued that the increased value of women could have a negative side, especially in rural society; increased female value may not benefit the woman herself, but rather the males around her. Her father, husband and in-laws all hold her value, so when her value increases her life is more controlled by them. Hudson and Den Boer (45) cite as examples the increase in kidnapping and trafficking of women that has been reported from many part of Asia, as well as the recent large increases in dowry prices in parts of India.

The Solutions

Governments in affected countries are taking action. Nothing can realistically be done in the short-term to reduce the current excess of young males, but much can be done to reduce sex selection now and this will benefit the next generation. China has set an ambitious, but almost certainly unachievable, target: to lower the sex ratio to normal by 2010 (62). In China and India, laws forbidding infanticide, abandonment and neglect of female children already exist but need to be strictly enforced. For trafficking and kidnapping, penalties are harsh (people-trafficking is a capital crime in China) but detection is difficult. Sex-selective abortion, however, is carried out by medical personnel in hospitals and clinics and enforcement of the law banning the practice should be straight forward. Stricter enforcement has been successful in reducing the sex ratio in South Korea, where in 1991eight physicians in Seoul had their licenses suspended for performing sex determination. In the following year, the sex ratio in Seoul fell from 117 to 113 suggesting that this punitive action had a deterrent effect for other physicians (31). Other countries could learn from this example.

Other measures include public awareness campaigns, which should focus on the problems facing young men in finding brides. More importantly, equal social and economic rights for males and females must be guaranteed, for example, in relation to rights of inheritance. Basic health care should be available free of charge, so that parents are not deterred by financial constraints from seeking health care for their daughters. In addition, special supportive measures should be provided for families with no sons, to ensure protection for parents in old age.

The Future

Although the effects of male surplus will be a major problem for several Asian countries over the next two to three decades, there are indications that the situation may then improve. In South Korea, the sex ratio has already declined and gender preference data from China are also encouraging. In a recent national survey, 37% of the Chinese women surveyed (predominantly younger, urban women) claimed to have no gender preference and 45% said the ideal family consisted of one boy and one girl (Table 3). Almost equal numbers of the women expressed a preference for one girl as for one boy (63).

Table 3: Gender Preferences of Chinese Women of Reproductive Age in 2001 (n=39,344)

No. of Boys	No. of Girls	n	%
0	1	2,323	5.9
0	2	267	0.7
1	0	2,218	5.6
1	1	17,882	45
1	2	254	0.6
2	0	274	0.7
2	1	1,123	2.8
2	2	566	1.4
No gender preference		14,437	37

Adapted from reference 60.

There are, therefore, clear indications that the essential fundamental change in attitudes is starting to happen. We believe that both the population sex ratio and the sex ratio at birth will gradually decline over the next two to three decades in these high-sex-ratio countries; however, the damage for a large number of today's young men and boys has already been done.

(Therese Hesketh, Institute of Child Health, University College London, 30 Guildford Street, London WCI N1EH, United Kingdom and

Zhu Wei Xing, Department of Public Health, Zhejiang Normal University, 299 Beishan Road, Jinhua 321004, People's Republic of China.)

References

1. Central Intelligence Agency (2005) *The World Factbook.* Available at *www.cia.gov/publications/factbook.* Accessed February 1, 2005.
2. Sen, A. (2003) *Br. Med. J.* 327, 1297-1298.

3. Merli, M. G. & Raftery, A. E. (2000) *Demography* 37, 109-126.
4. Campbell, R. B. (2001) *Hum. Biol.* 73, 605-610.
5. Coale, A. (1991) *Popul. Dev. Rev.* 3, 518.
6. Dickson, J. D. (1979) *Ann. Hum. Genet.* 40, 205-212.
7. James, W. H. (1987) *Hum. Biol.* 59, 721-725.
8. Teitelbaum, M. S. (1970) *J. Biosoc. Sci. Suppl.* 2, 61-71.
9. Ulizzi, L. & Zonta, L. A. (1995) *Hum. Biol.* 67, 59-67.
10. Graffellman, J. (2000) *Hum. Biol.* 72, 433-435.
11. MacMahon, B. & Pugh, T. F. (1954) *Am. Hum.Genet.* 7, 284-292.
12. Mathews, T. J. & Hamilton, B. E. (2005) *Natl. Vital Stat. Rep.* 53, 1-17.
13. Ellis, L. & Bonin, S. (2004) *Soc. Sci. Inf.* 43, 115-122.
14. Polasek, O. (2006) *Eur. J. Epidemiol.* 21, 61-64.
15. Saadat, M. & Ansari-Lari, M. (2002) *J. Epidemiol. Community Health* 56, 622-623.
16. Bisioli, C. (2004) *Hum. Reprod.* 19, 218-219.
17. Guerrero, R. (1974) *N. Engl. J. Med.* 29, 1056-1059.
18. James, W. H. (2003) *Hum. Reprod.* 18, 1133-1134.
19. Zorn, B., Sucur, V., Stare, J. & Meden-Vrtovec, H. (2002) *Hum. Reprod.* 17, 3173-3177.
20. Saadat, M. & Ansari-Lari, M. (2004) *Hum. Re-prod.* 19, 465.
21. Sen, A. K. (1992) *Br. Med. J.* 304, 586-587.
22. Waldron, I. (1993) *Soc. Sci. Med.* 36, 451-462.
23. Arnold, F. (1987) *Popul. Bull. UN* 23, 44-55.
24. Basu, A. (1989) *Popul. Stud.* 34, 93-210.
25. Coale, A. & Banister, J. (1996) *Proc. Am. Philos. Soc.* 140, 421-450.
26. Arnold, F., Choe, M. K. & Roy, T. K. (1998) *Popul. Stud.* 52, 301-315.
27. Leone, T., Matthews, Z. & Dalla-Zuanna, G. (2003) *Int. Fam. Plan. Perspect.* 29, 69-75.
28. Klasen, S. & Wink, C. (2002) *Popul. Dev. Rev.* 28, 285-312.
29. Gu, B. & Roy, K. (1995) *Asia Pac. Popul. J.* 10, 17-42.
30. Klasen, S. (1994) *World Dev.* 22, 944-948.
31. Park, C. B. & Cho, N. H. (1995) *Popul. Dev. Rev.* 21, 59-84.
32. Murthi, M., Guio, A. C. & Dreze, J. (1995) *Popul. Dev. Rev.* 21, 745-782.
33. Hill, K. & Upchurch, D. M. (1995) *Popul. Dev. Rev.* 21, 127-151.

34. Chen, L. C., Huq, E. & D'Souza, S. (1981) *Popul. Dev. Rev.* 7, 55-70.

35. Hazarika, G. (2000) *J. Dev. Stud.* 37, 73-92.

36. Li, J. (2004) *Soc. Sci. Med.* 59, 695-708.

37. Arnold, F., Kishor, S. & Roy, T. K. (2002) *Popul. Dev. Rev.* 28, 759-785.

38. Hesketh, T. & Zhu, W. X. (1997) *Br. Med. J.* 314, 1685-1687.

39. Jha, P., Kumar, R., Vasa, P., Dhingra, N., Thiruch-elvam, D. & Moineddin, R. (2006) *Lancet* 367, 211-218.

40. US Census Bureau (2005) *International Data Base: Online Demographic Aggregation.* Available at *www.census.gov/ipc/www/idbnew.html.* Accessed March 1, 2006.

41. Miller, B. D. (2001) *Am. Anthropol.* 103, 1083-1095.

42. Office of the Registrar General, India (New Delhi) (2001) *Census of India 2001: Provisional Population Totals.* Available at *www.censusindia.net/results.* Accessed March 1, 2006.

43. Hesketh, T., Li, L. & Zhu, W. X. (2005) *N. Engl. J. Med.* 353, 1171-1176.

44. Kang, C. & Wang, Y. (2003) in *Theses Collection of 2001 National Family Planning and Reproductive Health Survey* (China Population Publishing House, Beijing) pp. 88-98.

45. Hudson V. & Den Boer, A. M. (2004) *Bare Branches: The Security Implications of Asia's Surplus Male Population* (MIT Press, Cambridge, MA).

46. Hudson, V. & Den Boer, A. (2002) *Int. Secur.* 26, 5-38.

47. Zeng, Y., Tu, P., Gu, B., Xu, Y., Li, B. & Li, Y. (1993) *Popul. Dev. Rev.* 19, 283-302.

48. Zhang, P. (1990) *Chinese J. Popul. Sci.* 2, 87-97. 49. Li, N., Tuljapurkar, S. & Feldman, M. (1995) *Chinese J. Popul. Sci.* 7, 213-221.

50. Messner, S. F. & Sampson, R. J. (1991) *Soc. Forces* 69, 693-713.

51. Oldenberg, P. (1992) *Econ. Polit. Wkly.* 27, 2657-2662.

52. Ullman, J. B. & Fidell, L. S. (1989) in *Gender in Transition: A New Frontier,* ed. Offerman-Zuckerberg, J. (Plenum, New York), pp. 174-175.

53. Dreze, J. & Keher, R. (2000) *Popul. Dev. Rev.* 26, 335-352.

54. Li, Q. (April 5, 2001) Migrants blamed for crime wave. *China Daily.*

55. The National HIV Sentinel Surveillance Group (2001) *National Sentinel Surveillance Data for HIV Infection in China for 2000* (Ministry of Public Health, Beijing).

56. Dandona, R., Dandona, L., Kumar, G. A., Gutierrez, J. P., McPherson, S., Samuels, F. & Bertozzi, S. M. (2006) *BMC Int. Health Hum. Rights* 6, 5.

57. Hesketh, T., Zhang, J. & Qiang, D. J. (2005) *AIDS Care* 17, 958-966.

58. Tucker, J. D., Henderson, G. E., Wang, T. F., Huang, Y. Y., Parish, W., Pan, S. M., Chen, X. S. & Cohen, M. S. (2005) *AIDS* 19, 539-547.

59. Zhao, G. M. (2003) *Crim. Justice* 3, 83-102.

60. Sen, S. & Nair, P. M. (2004) *A Report on Trafficking in Women and Children in India 2002-2003* (Institute of Social Sciences, New Delhi).

61. United Nations Office on Drugs and Crime (2006) *Trafficking in Persons: Global Patterns.* Available at *www.unodc.org/unodc/trafficking/persons/report/2006-04.html.* Accessed February 1, 2006.

62. *People's Daily* (July 15, 2004). Available at *http://english.peopledaily.com.cn/200407/15/eng20040715/149701.html.* Accessed February 1, 2006.

63. Ding, Q. J. & Hesketh, T. (May 11, 2006) *Br. Med. J. 10.1136/bmj.38775.672662.80.*

4

Missing Women and Bare Branches

Gender Balance and Conflict

Valerie M Hudson and Andrea M den Boer

The two areas of the world where such imbalances have become fairly significant in the last five decades are: Russia and several Warsaw Pact nations where, there are deficit adult males and Asia—particularly India, China and Pakistan where, there is a deficit of women, including female infants and children. In societies, crime rates will increase, rate of drug use, drug smuggling, weapon smuggling, trafficking and prostitution will increase. The society may develop domestic and international markets that kidnap and trafficking in women within the country and across the borders.

The emerging subfield of "security demographics" examines the linkages between population dynamics and the security trajectories of nation-states. For the last 5 to 10 years, researchers have examined the security aspects of such topics as the demographic transition, the sub-replacement birth rates of developed economies, the proportion of young men as compared to older men in the

---

Source: Environmental Change and Security Program Report Issue 11, Woodrow Wilson Center: www.wilsoncenter.org/topics/pubs/Hudson&denBoer.pdf

population, the effects of legal and illegal immigration and the effects of pandemics such as AIDS and drug-resistant tuberculosis. We hope to add the variable of gender balance to the discussion: are societies with an abnormal ratio between men and women less secure?

Missing Women

In two areas of the world such imbalances have become fairly significant in the last half-century: 1) Russia and several former Warsaw Pact nations, where we find a deficit of adult males[1]; and 2) Asia—particularly India, China, and Pakistan—where we find a deficit of women, including female infants and children. We will let other scholars research the link between a deficit of males and national security. Our research, as explained in *Bare Branches: The Security Implications of Asia's Surplus Male Population* (MIT Press, 2004), focuses on the deficit of females in Asia. Standard demographic analysis readily confirms this abnormal deficit[2]. If we compare overall population sex ratios, the ratio for, say, Latin America is 98 males per 100 females (using 2000 US Census Bureau figures), but the corresponding figure for Asia is 104.4 males per 100 females. But one must also keep in mind the sheer size of Asia's population: India and China alone comprise approximately 38 percent of the world's population. Thus, the overall sex ratio of the world is 101.3, despite the fact that the ratios for the rest of the world (excluding Oceania) range from 93.1 (Europe) to 98.9 (Africa).

Birth sex ratios in several Asian countries are outside of the established norm of 105-107 boy babies born for every 100 girl babies. The Indian government's estimate of its birth sex ratio is approximately 113 boy babies born for every 100 girl babies, with some locales recording ratios of 156 and higher (India Registrar General, 2001). The Chinese government states that its birth sex ratio

---

1 In Russia and its former satellites, drug and alcohol abuse, as well as tuberculosis and AIDS, have dramatically increased the mortality rate for adult males—recent US Census Bureau (2005) figures estimate that there are 10 million fewer men than women in Russia alone. This, in turn, has fueled female emigration, supporting not only to a vigorous "mail-order bride" business, but also increasingly sophisticated and far-flung transnational prostitution and human trafficking networks.

2 There are established ranges of normal variation in overall population sex ratios, as well as early childhood and birth sex ratios. These ratios are adjusted for country-specific circumstances such as, for example, maternal mortality rates and infant mortality rates. Using official census data, we can determine if there are fewer women than could reasonably be expected. Of course, there are perturbing variables: for example, many of the Gulf states have very abnormal sex ratios favoring males due to the high number of guest workers, predominantly male, that labor in the oil economies of these states. Once we take these types of factors into account, we find that the deficit of females in Asia is a real phenomenon (Hudson & den Boer, 2004).

is approximately 119, though some Chinese scholars have gone on record that the birth sex ratio is at least 121 (China State Statistical Bureau, 2001).[3] Again, in some locations, the ratio is higher; for example, the island of Hainan's birth sex ratio is 135. Other countries of concern include Pakistan, Bangladesh, Nepal, Bhutan, Taiwan, Afghanistan, and South Korea[4].

Another indicator of gender imbalance is early childhood mortality. Boys typically have a higher early childhood mortality rate, which virtually cancels out their numerical advantage by age five. Boys' higher mortality is tied to sex-linked genetic mutations such as hemophilia as well as higher death rates from common childhood diseases such as dysentery. However, in some of the Asian nations mentioned above, early childhood mortality rates for girls are actually higher than boys' (United Nations Population Division, 1998). Furthermore, orphanages house more girls than boys in these nations[5].

What forces drive the deficit of females in Asian nations such as India and China? Why are their birth sex ratios so abnormal? Why are early childhood mortality rates for girls higher than those for boys? Why are most children in orphanages—girls? How do we account for the disappearance of so many women—estimated conservatively at over 90 million missing women in seven Asian countries alone? (see Table 1)

Some scholars assert that there may be a physical cause at work preventing female births, such as the disease hepatitis B, antigens of which have been associated with higher birth sex ratios (Oster, 2005). While this may well be a contributing factor, it is worth considering the experience of the municipality of Shenzhen in southern China. Alarmed at the rising birth sex ratio which reached 118 in 2002, local officials instituted a strict crackdown on black market ultrasound clinics. Offering up to 2,000 yuan for tips, officials then vigorously prosecuted and imprisoned the owners and technicians. By 2004, the birth sex ratio had dropped to 108 ("Shenzhen's newborn sex ratio more balanced", 2005).

---

3 Additional information provided by the director of the Chinese Academy of Social Sciences via e-mail, concerning the *Nando Times* article, "China Reportedly Has 20 Percent More Males Than Females", dated January 7, 1999.

4 No data are available for North Korea.

5 Other statistics also factor into the observed gender imbalance. In the West, for example, male suicides far outnumber female suicides. But in countries with deficits of women, female suicides outnumber male suicides. In fact, approximately 55 percent of all female suicides in the world are Chinese women of childbearing age (Murray & Lopez, 1996).

Table 1: Number of Missing Women for Selected Asian Countries Using Census Data

Country	Year	Actual Number of Males	Actual Number of Females	Actual Sex Ratio	Expected Sex Ratio	Expected Number of Women	Missing Women
Afghanistan	2000	11,227,000	10,538,000	106.5	96.4	11,646,266	1,108,266
Bangladesh	2001	65,841,419	63,405,814	103.8	99.6	66,105,842	2,700,028
China	2000	653,550,000	612,280,000	106.7	100.1	652,897,103	40,617,103
India	2001	531,277,078	495,738,169	107.2	99.3	535,022,234	39,284,065
Pakistan	1998	68,873,686	63,445,593	108.6	99.2	69,429,119	5,983,526
South Korea	2000	23,068,181	22,917,108	100.7	100.0	23,068,181	151,073
Taiwan	2000	11,386,084	10,914,845	104.3	100.2	11,363,357	448,512
Total							90,292,573

Accounts such as this, support the thesis that, the modern gender imbalance in Asia, as with historical gender imbalances in Asia and elsewhere, is largely a man-made phenomenon[6]. Girls are being culled from the population, whether through prenatal sex identification and female sex-selective abortion, or through relative neglect compared to male offspring in early childhood (including abandonment) or through desperate life circumstances that might lead to suicide.

The gender imbalance in Asia is primarily the result of son preference and the profound devaluation of female life. This value ordering is not confined to Asia; why then, is the deficit of women found there almost exclusively? Historically, of course, the culling of girls was not confined to Asia; evidence for this practice can be found in every continent. And practices are changing in some Asian nations: Japan normalized its sex ratios in the 20th century and in South Korea, the deficit has been decreasing over time (Dickemann, 1975; South Korea National Statistics Office, 2001).

But this excellent question can only be answered through a multifactorial cultural analysis that examines variables such as religious prohibitions or sanctions; patrilocality (couples living with the husband's family); the duty of male offspring to support aged parents; dowry, hypergyny and caste purity in India; the effect of interventions such as China's one-child policy and the web of incentives and disincentives surrounding the issue of prenatal sex determination technology[7].

6 For more examples, please see Hudson and den Boer (2004).

7 For a more complete cultural analysis of these practices in Asia, please see Hudson and den Boer (2004), Bossen (2000), Miller (2001), and Sen (1990).

Bare Branches

What effect will this deficit of females have on the security trajectory of nations? Anthropologist Barbara D Miller (2001) has termed the preservation of a balanced sex ratio a "public good" that governments overlook at their peril. Will it matter to India and China that by the year 2020, 12-15 percent of their young adult males will not be able to "settle down" because, the girls who would have grown up to be their wives were disposed off by their societies instead? With each passing year between now and 2020 (or even further), both the proportion and the number of young adult males that exceed the number of young adult females in China and India will increase (Hudson & den Boer, 2004). The Chinese have a special term for such young men: *guang gun-er*, or "bare branches"—branches of the family tree that will never bear fruit, but which may be useful as "bare sticks", or clubs.

The Chinese elision between bare branches and truncheons echoes our argument: men who are not provided the opportunity to develop a vested interest in a system of law and order will gravitate toward a system based on physical force, in which they hold an advantage over other members of society. Furthermore, in a system with too few women, the men who marry are those with higher socio-economic status. The men unable to marry are poorer, less educated, less skilled, and less likely to be employed. These men are already at risk for establishing a system, based on physical force, in order to obtain by force, what they cannot obtain legitimately. Without the opportunity to establish a household, they may not transit from potential threats to potential protectors of society. The rate of criminal behaviour of unmarried men is many times higher than that of married men; marriage is a reliable predictor of a downturn in reckless, antisocial, illegal and violent behaviour by young adult males (Mazur & Michalek, 1998). If this transition cannot be effected for a sizeable proportion of a society's young men, the society is likely to become less stable[8].

---

[8] Note that this transition is also less likely in societies with a deficit of males; in such societies, men need not marry or form permanent attachments to obtain food, shelter, sexual services, domestic services, and so forth. In that respect, societies with too few men and societies with too many men share some characteristics. Furthermore, societies in which marriage age is generally delayed for men can also produce instability; for example, the average age at first marriage for men in Egypt is now 32 (Diane Singerman, personal communication, July 19, 2004).

Statistical evidence for the linkage between gender imbalance and conflict includes several excellent studies that have demonstrated a strong correlation between state-level sex ratios and state-level rates of violent crime in India (Oldenburg, 1992; Dreze & Khera, 2000). States with high sex ratios, such as Uttar Pradesh, have much higher violent crime rates than states with more normal sex ratios, such as Kerala. Historical case studies abound, since abnormal sex ratios are not a new phenomena. The 19th century Nien rebels came from a very poor region in China with a sex ratio of at least 129 men per 100 women. At first, relatively smaller groups of men coalesced to form smuggling and extortion gangs. Eventually, these gangs banded together to form larger armies, wresting territory from imperial control. It took the emperor years to subdue this rebellion.

We must not overlook sociological theory and experimental evidence, as well. For example, scholars have studied the behaviour of unattached young males, noting their propensity to congregate with others like them and to engage in dominance displays in such groups. Sociologists have found that the "risky shift" in group behaviour, where a group is willing to take greater risks and engage in more reckless behaviour than an individual member of the group, is much more pronounced in groups comprised solely of unattached young adult males (Johnson, Stemler, & Hunter, 1977).

After examining the evidence, some predictions can be made for societies with rising sex ratios: crime rates will increase; the proportion of violent crime will increase; rates of drug use, drug smuggling, weapons smuggling, trafficking and prostitution will increase (see Hudson & den Boer, 2004). The society might develop domestic and international chattel markets that kidnap and traffic women within the country and across borders. For example, the shortage of marriage-age women in China is fueling a brisk business in trafficked brides from North Korea (Demick, 2003).

We must also examine the reaction of the government. Historically, we have found that, as governments become aware of the negative consequences of a growing number of bare branches, most governments are motivated to do something. In the past, "doing something" meant thinning the numbers of bare branches, whether through fighting, sponsoring the construction of large public works necessitating dangerous manual labour, exporting them to less populated areas, or co-opting them into the military or police. One 16th century Portuguese monarch sent his army, composed primarily of noble and non-noble bare branches, on one of the later crusades to avoid a crisis of governance; more than 25 percent of that army never returned and many others were seriously wounded (Boone, 1983, 1986).

We find that the need to control the rising instability created by the increasing numbers of bare branches has led governments to favour more authoritarian approaches to internal governance and less benign international presences. In many ways, a society's prospects for democracy and peace are diminished in step with the devaluation of daughters.

How will this play out in 21st century Asia? Gender imbalance does not cause war or conflict *per se*, but it can aggravate it. Will the internal instability caused by substantial numbers of bare branches (by 2020, 28 million in India—the same or more in China) overshadow external security concerns for the governments of these nations? Some potentially unstable situations spring to mind: the feuding countries of Pakistan and India have gender imbalances, as do China and Taiwan; and the resource-rich Russian Far East faces an influx of Chinese workers while Russia continues to lose men (Radyuhin, 2003).

How will gender imbalances affect the potential for democracy in China and the evolution of democracy in India? The gender imbalances of these two countries will not remain solely their problem, as alone they comprise more than one-third of the world's population. The status of women in these nations could become an important factor in both domestic and international security in Asia, with possible implications for the entire international system.

The Chinese government is acting on this linkage. In July 2004, they announced their desire to normalize the birth sex ratio by the year 2010 and in January 2005, they announced programs to provide old-age pensions to parents of girls. Only time will tell if these and other interventions will achieve their desired ends. In the meantime, the horse has left the barn for at least the next 20 years, for there is no way to undo the birth sex ratios of previous years.

Have these Asian nations discovered the value of female life too late? The whole world is waiting to see whether bare branches will be given the opportunity to grow again.

(Valerie M Hudson is a Professor of Political Science at Brigham Young University.

Andrea M den Boer is a Lecturer in Political Science at the University of Kent at Canterbury.)

References

Boone, James L. (1983). "Noble family structure and expansionist warfare in the Late Middle Ages". In Rada Dyson-Hudson & Michael A. Little (Eds.), *Rethinking human adaptation: Biological and cultural models* (pages 79-86). Boulder, CO: Westview.

Boone, James L. (1986). "Parental investment and elite family structure in preindustrial states: A case study of late medieval-early modern Portuguese genealogies". *American Anthropologist 88*(4), 859-878.

Bossen, Laurel. (2000). "Women and development". In Robert Gamer (Ed.), *Understanding Contemporary China* (pages 309-330). Boulder, CO: Lynne Rienner Publishers.

China State Statistical Bureau. (2001). *Major figures of the 2000 population census*. Beijing: China Statistics Press.

Demick, Barbara. (2003, August 18). "N. Korea's brides of despair". *Los Angeles Times*. Retrieved November 10, 2005, from *http://www2.gol.com/users/coynerhm/n_koreas_brides_of_despair.htm*

Dickemann, Mildred. (1975). "Demographic consequences of infanticide of man". *Annual Review of Ecology and Systematics 6*, 107-137.

Dreze, Jean, & Reetika Khera. (2000). "Crime, gender, and society in India: Insights from homicide data". *Population and Development Review* 26(2), 335-352.

Hudson, Valerie M., & Andrea M. den Boer. (2004). *Bare branches: The security implications of Asia's sur-plus male population.* Cambridge, MA: MIT Press.

India Registrar General. (2001). *Census of India, 2001, Series 1: India, Paper of 2001: Provisional population totals.* New Delhi, India: Office of the Registrar General.

Johnson, Norris R., James G. Stemler, & Deborah Hunter. (1977). "Crowd behavior as 'risky shift': A laboratory experiment". *Sociometry* 40(2), 183-187.

Mazur, Allan, & Joel Michalek. (1998). "Marriage, divorce, and male testosterone". *Social Forces,* 77 (1), 315-330.

McDonald, Hamish. (1991, December 26). "Unwelcome sex". *Far Eastern Economic Review* 154(52), 18-19.

Miller, Barbara D. (2001). "Female-selective abortion in Asia: Patterns, policies, and debates". *American Anthropologist* 103(4), 1083-1095.

Murray, Christopher J.L., & Alan D. Lopez (Eds.). (1996). *The global burden of disease: A comprehensive assessment of mortality and disability from diseases, injuries, and risk factors in 1990 and projected to 2020.* Cambridge, MA: Harvard University Press.

Oldenburg, Philip. (1992). "Sex ratio, son preference, and violence in India: A research note". *Economic and Political Weekly* 27(49-50), 2657-2662.

Oster, Emily. (2005, December). "Hepatitis B and the case of the missing women". *Journal of Political Economy* 113(6), 1163-1216. Retrieved November 4, 2005, from *http://www.people.fas.harvard.edu/~eoster/hepb.pdf*

Radyuhin, Vladamir. (2003, September 23). "A Chinese 'invasion'". *The Hindu.* Retrieved November 7, 2005, from *http://www.worldpress.org/Asia/1651.cfm#down*

"Shenzhen's newborn sex ratio more balanced". (2005, April 15). *Shenzhen Daily.* Retrieved November 10, 2005, from *english.people.com.cn/200504/15/ eng20050415_181218.html*

Sen, Amartya. (1990, December 20). "More than 100 million women are missing". *New York Review of Books* 37(20), 61-66.

South Korea National Statistics Office. (2001). *2001 report of the National Statistical Office of South Korea.* Seoul: National Statistics Office.

United Nations Population Division. (1998). *Too young to die: Genes or gender.* New York: United Nations.

United States Census Bureau. (2005). *International database summary demographic data for Russia.* Retrieved November 4, 2005, from *http://www.census.gov/cgi-bin/ipc/ idbsum.pl?cty=RS*

Security Concerns and Gender Imbalance

– Meenu Bhatnagar

According to the UN report "the preference for boys over girls is skewing the gender ratio imbalance in Asia". The social disturbance due to this imbalance is a matter of grave concern with regards to the security of the women. Traditionally and culturally preference for boys and girls as lesser mortal is deeply embedded in our society. There is a clear and marked demarcation in roles both boys and girls are to play.

Women are known as weaker sex. Firstly, the discrimination starts at birth and then continues throughout the life. Sex discrimination after the child is conceived is followed by abortion if the foetus is female. If the first child is girl then the second has to be a boy otherwise female foetuses are aborted. Sometimes, the desire for male child is so strong that female child is aborted without any remorse. Some of the reasons which need urgent attention are violence against women, prostitution, women trafficking, female literacy, urbanization, poverty and kidnapping women for marriages across regions.

To tackle the serious repercussion of gender ratio imbalance, efforts are being made by different governments to better the status of women in society. In India, several schemes like campaigns against female foeticide, strict implementation of Preconception and Prenatal Diagnostic Techniques (PCPNDT) Act 1994, Integrated Child Protection Scheme (ICPS) for protecting girl child and fundamental "cash transfer Scheme" for families to allow their daughters to live and thrive. Various conferences and seminars are held to spread the awareness to help change the mindset of people and society in general, which views sons as assets and daughters as liabilities. In the rural areas, cash incentives given to poor families having girl children have to guarantee that the birth would take place and registered, immunization would be completed, would be given education and marriage would take place only after she completes 18 years of age.

The efforts being made through policies, rules and regulation are to make sure that the girl child gets a fair chance to be born and the financial incentives are given as security to the families and the well-being of the girl child. Technological and academic advancements are slowly improving the status of women but it is a long way to go when women will be truly empowered and accorded an equal status as men.

(Meenu Bhatnagar is a Faculty Associate at Icfai Research Centre, Ahmedabad, Gujarat. She can be reached at meenub@ibsindia.org).

5

Gender Inequality

Is the National Population Policy's Objective of Two Child Norm Heading the Correct Way?

SR Patrikar, Col R Bhalwar, Col A Datta and DR Basannar

Background: Male preference is a well-known phenomena world wide from ancient ages. A descriptive study was carried out to assess the attitude of women towards the birth of a son, use of contraception methods and sex determination methods in a rural village named Kasurdi in Pune district.

Methods: Univariate analysis was carried out by considering each factor determining sex preference separately as well as using a Logistic Regression Model. Adequacy of fit of the model has also been tested.

Result and Conclusion: Out of 110 respondents interviewed, 62.7% felt that a male child is necessary in the family. Univariate analysis revealed that sex of the first child, concern undergone for second pregnancy with regards to sex of the child, number of children in the family and type of the family were the significant factors contributing to the son

Source: MJAFI 2008; 64: 221-3. Available at http://medind.nic.in/maa/t08/i3/maat08i3p221.pdf

preference. The analysis under the logistic regression model revealed that sex of the first child and concern undergone in second pregnancy with respect to the sex of the second child are the most dominating and significant factors in the causation of son preference. The difference between family sizes when compared with the sex of the first child, was statistically significant signifying that if the first child is a male then it hardly matters whether the second child is a male or female, but, if the sex of the first child is female then the families land up with a bigger family size. On an average, most of the respondents favour two children with an equal share of male and female children.

Introduction

Preference for male sex is a well-known phenomena from ages. India shares a distinctive feature of the South Asian population with regard to the sex ratio, with a century old deficit of females. The 2001 census shows a rise of six more females per 1000 males than the 927 of previous census. The fall in sex ratio of upto six years population is however continuing and the gender gap is expanding [1]. The census has revealed that the sex ratio in the age-group of upto six years in India has further gone down sharply from 945 females per 1000 males in 1991 to 927 in 2001. In a country like India which is undergoing demographic transition, sex ratio at birth in combination with the under enumeration of female births or excess female mortality throughout the life course, have a potentially large effect on the overall sex ratio [2]. In India, the preference for a son is very strong and has been frequently cited as one of the major obstacles for reducing the national fertility level [3, 4].

A descriptive study was undertaken to assess the attitude of women towards the birth of a son in a rural village Kasurdi in Pune. The study also assesses the knowledge and use of contraception methods and sex determination methods. This article seeks to analyse the transition in terms of family size, sex of the first child and sex preference in a set of rural women of Pune.

Material and Methods

Kasurdi village is situated around 40 kms from Pune. The total population of the village is 1796 consisting of 328 families. There were a total of 212 married females in the reproductive age group of 15 to 49 years. A pilot study was carried out to find the prevalence of son preference. The pilot study revealed the estimate of son preference to be nearly 70%. Thus, taking a prevalence of 70% with 5% precision on either side of the true value and 95% confidence interval with finite population correction, a sample size of 128 was decided and data was collected accordingly, using a structured questionnaire. The respondent was the female spouse in the reproductive age group. There were eight respondents without any children and ten respondents did not give complete information, therefore the data on 110 respondents was analysed. The respondents were interviewed about their socio-economic background, family size, practice of contraception and the use of sex determination methods. The preference for a son was assessed by getting the information whether the respondents felt that a male child is necessary in the family. The responses were obtained on various attributes like age, education, number of children, sex of first child, concern undergone with respect to the sex of the child during second pregnancy and the type of family. Responses were also sought regarding who should be responsible to take a decision of having a child and also, whether the lady's opinion is sought in the family at various levels. Respondents were also given a hypothetical situation to identify the exact or ideal number of children preferred by them and the sex composition of the children. All those who had completed their family size were asked to imagine backwards in time and those who had no children to have forward imagination. Univariate analysis was carried out by considering each factor separately. Son Preference was analysed using a Logistic Regression Model. Adequacy of fit of the model has also been tested.

Results

Out of 110 respondents interviewed 62.7% (95% confidence interval 53.41-71.38) felt that a male child is necessary. Univariate analysis for association between the attributes was carried out using chi square test. It revealed that sex of the first child, concern about sex of the child during second pregnancy, number of children and type of family were significant factors contributing to the preference of son ($p<0.001$), the details of which are given in Table 1.

Table 1: Univariate Analysis of Different Factors along with Odds Ratio and 95% Confidence Interval

Attributes	Having Son Preference	Odds Ratio Alongwith Significance Value	95% Confidence Interval
Age (in years)			
≤ 20	6	(p=0.11)	
20-30	39		
30-40	23		
>40	5		
Education			
Illiterate	27	(p=0.94)	
Pre-school	14		
Secondary	20		
SSC	12		
Number of children**			
≤ 2	15	3.92 (p=0.000)	(1.52, 10.28)
>2	50		
Occupation			
Employed	30	(p=0.17)	
Farmer	24		
House wife	19		
Sex of first child**			
Male	9	65.36 (p=0.0000)	(15.52, 310.67)
Female	59		
Concern during second pregnancy regarding sex of child**			
Yes	57	25.83 (p=0.0000)	(7.88, 89.80)
No	8		
Opinion asked in the family at all levels			
Yes	19	(p=0.18)	
No	54		
Type of family**			
Joint	32	(p=0.02)	(1.05, 7.80)
Nuclear	41		
Decision regarding child birth			
Both	25	(p=0.38)	
Husband	45		
In laws	3		

** $p<0.05$ (significant at 5% level of significance)

Concern about sex of the child during second pregnancy revealed that, sex of the first child is a significant factor (p<0.001). The analysis under the logistic regression model revealed that, sex of the first child and concern during second pregnancy with respect to the sex of the second child are the most dominating and significant factors in the causation of son preference (p<0.001). The maximum likelihood estimates of the parameters, the standard errors and the odds ratio along with 95% confidence interval under the logistic regression model are shown in Table 2.

Table 2: Parameters Estimated for the Son Preference by Logistic Regression

Variables	Estimate	Standard Error	Odds Ratio = e^{β}	95% CI
Age	-6.22	5.68	2.82	(0.02, 2.00)
Education	2.85	1.64	1.57	(0.71, 33.85)
Type of family	0.03	0.92	1.03	(0.14. 5.02)
Number of children	1.36	0.97	0.16	(0.57, 25.55)
Sex of first child**	2.60	0.78	13.52**	(1.57, 63.23)
Concern**	2.59	0.77	13.39**	(2.95, 60.81)
Opinion	0.57	1.03	1.77	(0.76, 4.06)
Responsible for child birth	-2.27	4.75	0.10	(0.05, 258.2)

** (p<0.05) Significant at 5% level of significance.

The goodness of fit test for the fitted model is carried out using the likelihood ratio test. The test statistic chi-square value was 5.09 with 8 degrees of freedom and p=0.75 which is not significant at 5% level of significance (p>0.05). Hence, it was concluded that, the logistic model is appropriate for the above analyses. The model summarizes the R Square value of 0.814 which implies that, more than 81% of the variation in the response (son preference) is explained by the model. Of the families who had first a female child, 79% had the family size of >2 children whereas, in families who had first male child, only 45% had >2 children. This difference was significant (p=0.000).

In the present study 66% of the respondents did not have any knowledge about the sex determination tests as against 34% who had some knowledge. 92% of these respondents who did not have knowledge regarding sex-determination did not approve of abortion. More than 8% of the respondents were ready to take as many pregnancies as required to have a male child. 46% of women were ready to take more than two chances as against 28% of the respondents who were not ready to take even a single chance for male child. As for the number of pregnancies for a girl child, a significant number (36%) of the respondents were not ready to take any chance, for fear of girl child. There were no respondents to take more than two chances for a girl child as compared to 26% for a male child. 90% of the respondents favoured two children and more than 77% agreed for one male and one female child, as the ideal sex combination in a family. One method of investigating the impact of sex preferences is by examining data related to sex composition of living children of couples who are currently practicing contraception. If son preference is important then, within any parity, those with one or more son/s would be more likely to be currently using some method of family planning as compared to those who have no son. Conversely, if the desire for a balanced sex composition affects fertility behaviour then within a given parity, couples that have had either all sons or daughters would be less likely to accept contraception, particularly sterilization, as compared to those who have had children of both sexes. In this study, 54% respondents had knowledge of the different methods of contraception but only 24% used contraception. The source of the knowledge regarding the contraceptive methods were doctors, health workers, TV and radio. 74% felt that birth control is good. Many of the respondents agreed that, permanent sterilization is good after completing the desired family size. Though the respondents agreed to spacing and restricting the family size, the contraceptive use was very less.

Discussion

It can be observed that the odds ratio computed using univariate analysis and logistic regression analysis differ. In case of univariate analysis number of children, sex of first child, concern during second pregnancy regarding sex of child and type of family were found to be significant, whereas in case of logistic regression analysis, sex of first child and concern during second pregnancy regarding sex of the child were found significant. The above analyses lead us to the conclusion that, sex of the first child plays an important role in sex preference. Conversely, if the first child is a female child then the families have a bigger family size and the concern regarding sex of second child is very high, which is in agreement with other similar studies [5].

The decline in the female sex ratio of our country in the twentieth century is disturbing [6]. In India, considering the high level of female child mortality, a lower level of child sex ratio of 935 girls per 1000 boys is considered reasonable. Ratio below this should be viewed with concern [7]. The decline in juvenile sex ratio over the years in India has shifted the concern from overall sex ratio to the sex ratio of child population [8-10]. The National Population Policy aims at achieving a total fertility rate <2.1 which is equivalent to attaining approximately two child norm [11]. While achieving this target, there is also a need to emphasise on programmes and policies that actively improve the status of women and change of attitude towards the female child.

Conflicts of Interest

None identified.

Intellectual Contribution of Authors

Study Concept: SR Patrikar, Col R Bhalwar

Drafting & Manuscript Revision: SR Patrikar, Col R Bhalwar, Col A Datta, DR Basannar *Statistical Analysis*: SR Patrikar, DR Basannar *Study Supervision*: SR Patrikar, Col R Bhalwar, Col A Datta.

(SR Patrikar, Lecturer (Statistic and Demography), Col R Bhalwar, Professor and Head, Col A Datta, Associate Professor and DR Basannar, Sc 'E', Department of Community Medicine (PSM) Armed Forces Medical College, Pune.)

References

1. Office of the Registrar General, India. Census of India 2001.
2. Agnihotri SB. Missing Females: Diaggregated Analysis. *Economic and Political Weekly* 1996; 31: 2074-84.
3. Rajaretnam T, Deshpande RV. The effect of sex preferences on contraceptive use and fertility in rural South India. *International Family Planning Perspectives 1994*; 20: 88-95.

4. Nag M. Sex preferences in Bangladesh, India and Pakistan and its effect on fertility. *Demography India* 1992; 20: 163-85.

5. Gangopadhyay BMS, Das DN. Transition of preferred sex combination of children and family size: An analysis of the behavioural mechanism. *Journal of Family Welfare* 1996; 40: 57-66.

6. Visaria PM. The sex Ratio of the population of India and Pakistan and Regional Variations During 1901-61. In: Bose A, editor. Patterns of Population Change in India 1951-61. Bombay: Allied Publishers, 1967; 334-71.

7. Gender Issues in Population Studies: Evidences from India. International Institute of Population Studies, Mumbai First edition November 2004; 68-9.

8. Kishore J. Vanishing Girl Child. 1st ed. Century Publications: New Delhi, 2005.

9. India National Family Health Survey 1992-3. International Institute for Population Studies, Mumbai 1995.

10. Rangamuthia M, Cuoe MK, Arnold F, Roy TK. Son preference and its effect on fertility in India. National Family Health Survey Subject Reports Number 3; 1997.

11. Ministry of Health and Family Welfare (MOHFW) 2000. National Population Policy 2000 report, New Delhi.

Section II

Experiences

6

How does Son Preference Affect Populations in Asia

Sidney B Westley and Minja Kim Choe

The preference for sons has deep social, economic and cultural roots in many East and South Asian societies. Historically, son preference has resulted in unusually high death rates for female infants and girls. Over the past 30 years, the introduction of prenatal screening technologies combined with widespread access to abortion has made possible the selective abortion of female foetuses. Resulting gender imbalances have led to concerns that a shortage of women will make it difficult for men to find wives. The Chinese, Indian and South Korean governments have responded by making prenatal screening for sex identification illegal. China and India have also launched campaigns to improve attitudes toward girl children, and both countries offer small allowances to some parents of girls. Experience in South Korea indicates that sex-selective abortion peaks and then declines with social and economic modernization. Population projections and survey data suggest that falling fertility and women's reluctance to marry have a much larger effect than sex-selective abortion on the availability of women in the marriage market.

Source: www.eastwestcenter.org © East-West Center. Reprinted with permission. How Does Son Preference Affect Populations in Asia, by Sidney B. Westley and Minja Kim Choe, originally appeared in the AsiaPacific Issues series (No. 84, September 2007, East-West Center, Honolulu).

Introduction

In China, the peasants have a saying: "The birth of a boy is welcomed with shouts of joy and firecrackers, but when a girl is born, the neighbours say nothing"[1]. In India, until recently, billboard messages promised: "Invest Rs.(rupees)500 now, save 50,000 later", encouraging prospective parents to abort female foetuses in order to avoid future dowry expenses[2]. The preference for sons reflected in these quotes has deep social and cultural roots in some East and South Asian societies. Male children carry on the family name, inherit the family property, and play a special role in family traditions. In Hindu families, a son lights the funeral pyre when his parents die. In countries with a strong Confucian influence, such as China and the Republic of Korea (South Korea), family rituals must be led by the eldest son of the most recent male ancestor. If no sons are born, the family dies.

Powerful economic factors also support son preference. In many Asian societies, married sons are expected to live with ageing parents and provide financial support. By contrast, when a woman marries, she joins her husband's household and does not normally contribute to the support of her own parents. Her marriage itself may impose a financial burden—through expectations of a large celebration, as in South Korea or expensive dowry payments, as in India.

In South Korea until very recently, family law reinforced Confucian traditions of son preference[3]. The Korean Civil Code of 1958 stipulated, among other things, that families must be headed by eldest sons, that inheritance is exclusively through the male line, that women are transferred to their husbands' family register upon marriage, and that children belong to the family of the father. Not until 2005 did the Supreme Court abolish the legal basis for male dominance over South Korean families. In China and India, by contrast, governments in

---

1 Isabelle Attané, "Gender Discriminations at Early Stages of Life in China: Evidence from 1990 and 2000 Population Censuses", in *Gender Discrimination Among Young Children in Asia*, eds. Isabelle Attané and Jacques Véron (Pondicherry, India: French Institute of Pondicherry, 2005).

2 Robert D. Retherford and Tarun K. Roy, "Effects of Family Composition on Sex-Selective Abortion in Punjab, India", *Genus 60*, Nos. 3-4 (2004): 71-97.

3 Woojin Chung and Monica Das Gupta, "Why is Son Preference Declining in South Korea? The Role of Development and Public Policy and the Implications for China and India" (Paper presented at the annual meeting of the Population Association of America, New York, March 29-31, 2007).

the modern era have consistently promoted gender equality, although with varying levels of forcefulness.

In its most extreme manifestation, son preference can affect how many boys and girls survive into adulthood and even how many boys and girls are born.

In most human populations, women give birth to slightly more boys than girls. The result is an average ratio of 104 to 106 males for every 100 females born. Within each age group, slightly more men die than women, so that at some point in adulthood the number of men and women becomes roughly balanced. If son preference alters these general features of human biology—so that many more boys are born than girls and more boys than girls survive to adulthood—the result will be an unusually large proportion of men in an adult population.

This article summarizes birth and death rates for boys and girls, explores some of the social consequences of unbalanced sex ratios and describes recent policy responses of Asian governments. The focus is on three Asian populations that have shown strong evidence of gender imbalance in their birth rates—South Korea, China and the north Indian state of Punjab.

High Death Rates for Girls

Nobel Prize-winning economist Amartya Sen was one of the first to call attention to Asia's "missing women". Using population data from the mid-1980s, he estimated that India and China alone had "lost" more than 80 million women and girls due to unusually high female mortality[4]. Around the world, death rates between birth and age five are higher for boys than for girls. But the balance is reversed in four Asian countries—China, India, Nepal, and Pakistan[5]. In the early 1960s, girls in South Korea also had higher death rates than boys[6], but today under-five mortality is the same for both sexes.

Unusually high death rates for girls probably result primarily from favoritism toward boys in food allocation, prevention of diseases and accidents, and

---

4 Amartya Sen, "The Many Faces of Gender Inequality", *The New Republic*, September 17, 2001, 35-40.

5 United Nations Population Division, World Population Prospects: The 2006 Revision, Population Database, *http://esa.un.org/unpp/index.asp?panel=2* (China, India, Nepal, and Pakistan; accessed March 20, 2007).

6 Minja Kim Choe, "Sex Differentials in Infant and Child Mortality in Korea", *Social Biology* 34, Nos. 1-4 (1987): 12-25.

treatment of illness[7]. The highest death rates tend to be for girls with older sisters. Findings from Punjab provide a striking example. Among children surviving until their first birthday, death rates from ages one to four were higher for girls than for boys in every type of family[8], but they were especially high for girls with older sisters (Figure 1). In a society that prefers sons, the youngest daughter in a family of girls is at a particularly severe disadvantage.

Figure 1: Death Rates at Ages 1 to 4 Years for the Youngest Children in Family, Punjab State, India, 1982-83 to 1992-93

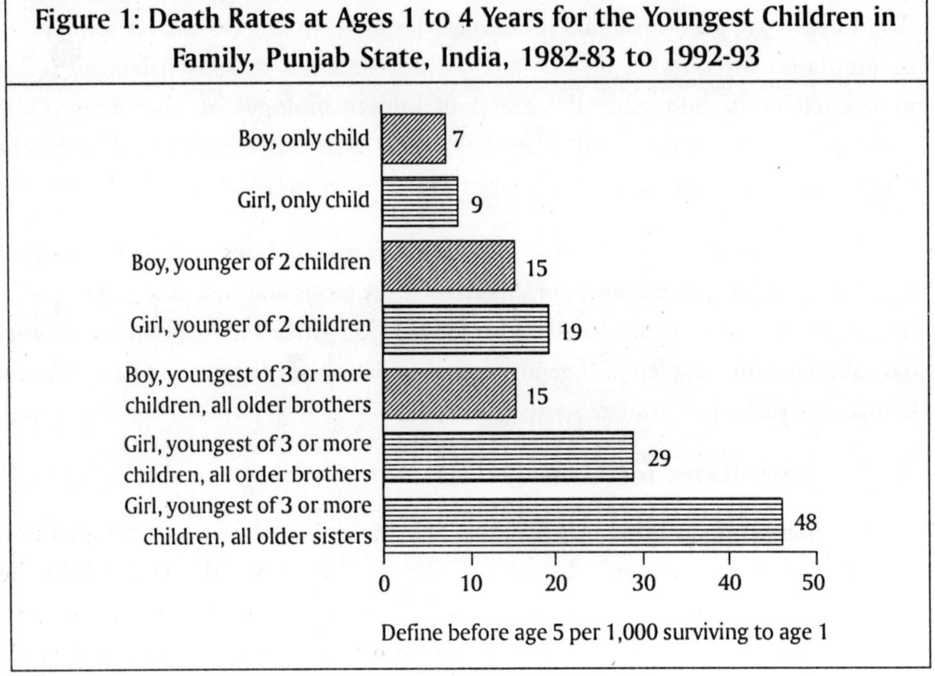

The Advent of Sex-Selective Abortion

During the past 30 years, some societies in Asia began to show an unprecedented preponderance of male births. In South Korea, China, Hong Kong, Taiwan, Singapore, and some of the northern and western states of India, the introduction of technologies to determine the sex of unborn fetuses combined with the

7 Arvind Pandey, Minja Kim Choe, Norman Y. Luther, Damodar Sahu, and Jagdish Chand, "Infant and Child Mortality in India", *National Family Health Survey Subject Reports*, No. 11 (Mumbai: International Institute for Population Sciences; Honolulu: East-West Center, 1998).

8 Fred Arnold, Minja Kim Choe, and T.K. Roy, "Son Preference, the Family-Building Process and Child Mortality in India", *Population Studies* 52 (1998): 301-315.

widespread availability of abortion made it possible for couples who wanted a son to selectively abort female foetuses.

Foetal screening technologies were introduced in several Asian countries during the 1970s. Three methods are currently available: ultrasound, amniocentesis, and chorionic villi sampling. Ultrasound is the safest, least expensive and the most widely used, but the test is not accurate until the second trimester of pregnancy, resulting in late abortions with some increased risk to the mother.

Ultrasound equipment was first mass-produced in South Korea in the mid-1980s and is now available in clinics and hospitals throughout the country. China began manufacturing ultrasound machines in 1979. Twenty years later, the largest ultrasound manufacturer in the country had the capacity to produce 5,000 machines a year[9]. Today, nearly every county and township hospital and family planning service center in China is equipped with modern ultrasound facilities, operated by skilled technicians and ultrasound is also available in many private clinics. In India, ultrasound equipment is also widely accessible in hospitals and private clinics, and in some rural areas prenatal sex identification using ultrasound has even been offered illegally in travelling vans.

This technology has become available in societies where abortion is legal and widely practiced. In South Korea, the Maternal and Child Health Act of 1973 legalized induced abortion, but only under quite restrictive conditions[10]. Nonetheless, abortion is one of the most common methods of fertility control, used as a backup method in case of contraceptive failure. The proportion of pregnancies terminated by induced abortion reached a peak in 1979, at 43 abortions for every 100 known pregnancies.

Induced abortion has been legal in China since August 1953 when the central government issued the Regulation on Contraception and Induced Abortion to secure the rights of women in healthcare and working conditions[11].

---

9 Chu Junhong, "Prenatal Sex Determination and Sex-Selective Abortion in Rural Central China", *Population and Development Review* 27, No. 2 (2001): 259-81.

10 Minja Kim Choe and Seung-Kwon Kim, "Pregnancy Wastage among Married Women in South Korea", *Asian Population Studies* 3, No. 1 (March 2007): 37-55.

11 Chui Fengyuan, "Population Policy of China", in *Symposium of Chinese Population Science* (in Chinese) (Beijing: China Academic Press, 1981).

Abortion ratios started to climb in the 1970s, reaching a peak of 41 abortions for every 100 known pregnancies in 1983.[12]

In India, abortion has been legal since the 1971 passage of the Medical Termination of Pregnancy Act. Revised in 1975, the Act allows abortion for five reasons, including contraceptive failure—in effect, legalizing abortion on demand. Reported legal abortion rates are very low, however. One estimate for 2000 gives a ratio of 3 abortions for every 100 pregnancies[13]. Yet, given India's large population, the absolute number of abortions is substantial. In their work on the Indian national health survey, Robert D Retherford and T K Roy estimated that 5 to 6 million pregnancies are aborted every year[14].

Although foetal screening for sex identification is illegal in all three countries, it appears to have been heavily used in South Korea in the past and is still heavily used in China and some of the northern and western states of India. It is difficult to obtain direct evidence of a practice that is illegal, but in South Korea, a conservative estimate suggested that more than 35,000 foetuses were screened for sex identification in 1990.[15] Comparing sex ratios at birth for women who did or did not receive ultrasound or amniocentesis during pregnancy, demographers Fred Arnold, Sunita Kishor, and T K Roy estimate conservatively that about 106,000 female foetuses are screened and aborted in India every year[16]. The indirect, but compelling, evidence for foetal sex screening in all three countries, however, is the unnatural preponderance of male births.

Distortions in Male and Female Births

In South Korea and China, the number of boys born compared with the number of girls—the sex ratio at birth—began to rise abruptly in the 1980s (Table 1). In South Korea, the sex ratio at birth peaked at 116 in 1990 and has since declined.

---

12 William Robert Johnston, "Historical Abortion Statistics, PR China", *Johnston's Archives, http://www.johnstons archive.net/policy/abortion/ab-prchina* (accessed March 29, 2007).

13 Ibid.

14 Robert D Retherford and T K Roy, "Factors Affecting Sex-Selective Abortion in India and 17 Major States", *National Family Health Survey Subject Reports*, No. 21 (Mumbai: International Institute for Population Sciences; Honolulu: East-West Centre, 2003).

15 Chai Bin Park and Nam Hoon Cho, "Consequences of Son Preference in a Low Fertility Society: Imbalance of the Sex Ratio at Birth in Korea", *Population and Development Review* 21, No. 1 (1995): 59-84.

16 Fred Arnold, Sunita Kishor, and T K Roy, "Sex-Selective Abortions in India", *Population and Development Review* 28, No. 4 (2002): 759-85.

In China, the sex ratio at birth reached 124 in 1995 and may now be stabilizing or coming down slightly. Between 1984 and 1998, the sex ratio at birth in Punjab was 116.[17]

Table 1: Reported Sex Ratios at Birth by Birth Order, South Korea and China, 1982-2000

Year	Country	All Births	1st Born	2nd Born	3rd Born and Above
1985	S. Korea	109	106	108	134
	China	111	106	116	—
1990	S. Korea	116	108	117	192
	China	111	105	121	127
1995	S. Korea	113	106	112	180
	China	124	109	160	140
2000	S. Korea	110	106	107	144
	China	120	107	152	159
2005	S. Korea	108	105	106	128
	China	121	108	143	153

Note: Sex ratio at birth is defined as the number of boys born for every 100 girls.

Sources: For South Korea, KOSIS (Korean Statistical Information Service), http://www.kosis.kr/index.html (in Korean) (accessed July 5, 2007). For China, data for 1985 from State Statistical Bureau, People's Republic of China, Statistical Yearbook of China 1985 (Oxford: Oxford University Press, 1985); data for 1990 from National Population Census Office under the State Council and Department of Population Statistics, National Bureau of Statistics of China, Tabulation of the 1990 Population Census of the People's Republic of China [in Chinese] (Beijing: China Statistical Publishing House, 1993); data for 1995 from Department of Population, Social, Science, and Technology Statistics, National Bureau of Statistics of China, Women and Men in China [in Chinese] (Beijing: China Statistics Press, 2004); data for 2000 from Population Census Office under the State Council and Department of Population, Social, Science, and Technology Statistics, National Bureau of Statistics of China, Tabulation on the 2000 Population Census of the People's Republic of China [in Chinese] (Beijing: China Statistics Press, 2002); and data for 2005 from One-Percent Population Sample Survey Office under the State Council and Department of Population and Employment Statistics, National Bureau of Statistics of China, Tabulation of the 2005 National One-Percent Population Sample Survey [in Chinese] (Beijing: China Statistics Press, 2007).

The evidence for sex-selective abortion is particularly striking when sex ratios at birth are broken down by birth order. In 1990, the sex ratio for third and subsequent children in South Korea was 192, indicating that nearly two boys were born at this birth order for every girl. In China, the sex ratio for third and subsequent children reached 159 in 2000.

[17] Fred Arnold, Sunita Kishor, and T K Roy, "Sex-Selective Abortions in India", *Population and Development Review* 28, No. 4 (2002): 759-85.

Between 1984 and 1998 in Punjab, the sex ratio at birth for second children was 101 if the first child was a son and 139 if the first child was a daughter[18]. For third children in families that already had two daughters, the sex ratio at birth was 172. Interestingly, in families that already had two sons and no daughters, the sex ratio for third children was 90, indicating some sex-selective abortion of male foetuses.

Even in societies that strongly prefer sons, women still want daughters. In India, women interviewed during 1998-99 ideally wanted two or three children. Eighty-five percent wanted at least one son, but 80 percent wanted at least one daughter[19]. The ideal family for many Indian women would be one or two boys and one girl.

Today in South Korea, there is evidence that sex-selective abortion is dying out. The sex ratio at birth is returning to normal levels and women's attitudes appear to be changing. In 1985, 48 percent of South Korean women felt that they "must have a son"; by 2003, the proportion had dropped to 17 percent[20]. A comparison of survey results from 1991 and 2003 found a steep drop in the proportion of women expressing strong son preference in every age group, every area of residence and every income and education level, indicating that this change in attitude is sweeping through the entire South Korean population. At the same time, the sex ratio at birth has been coming down (Table 1), and the abortion ratio has also declined—to 24 abortions for every 100 known pregnancies in 2003, the same as the 2002 estimate for the United States[21]. Although the trend started slightly later, abortion ratios have declined steadily in China, dropping from 41 abortions per 100 known pregnancies in 1983 to 27 in 2001.[22]

In Punjab, by contrast, women's stated preference for sons has been coming down, but sex ratios at birth have been going up[23]. It is not unusual for these two

---

18 Retherford and Roy, "Factors Affecting Sex-Selective Abortion".

19 International Institute for Population Sciences and ORC Macro, *National Family Health Survey (NFHS-2), 1998–99: India* (Mumbai: International Institute for Population Sciences, 2000).

20 Chung and Das Gupta, "Why is Son Preference Declining?"

21 Choe and Kim, "Pregnancy Wastage"; Guttmacher Institute, "Facts on Induced Abortion in the United States", *In Brief* (June 2006): 1-2.

22 Johnston, "Historical Abortion Statistics".

23 Retherford and Roy, "Effects of Family Composition"; International Institute for Population Sciences, *2005-2006 National Family Health Survey (NFHS-3): Fact Sheet: Punjab (Provisional Data)* (Mumbai: International Institute for Population Sciences, 2007), *http://www.nfhsindia.org/pdf/PJ.pdf* (accessed July 8, 2007).

phenomena to move in opposite directions, as fewer women feel strongly that they must have a son while, at the same time, more women gain access to sex-selection technology. Eventually, as attitudes change, the sex ratio at birth should also start to go down.

Son Preference and Fertility

Preference for a particular family configuration, which is most often a preference for sons, can have a strong effect on fertility. This is because, couples who have all the sons they want will use contraception to prevent additional pregnancies, while couples who are hoping for a son will keep on having children.

When women in Punjab were surveyed in the early 1990s, just over one-fourth (29 percent) of those with two sons and one daughter went on to have another child. But women with three daughters were strongly motivated to keep trying for a son: Nearly three-fourths (74 percent) of this group went on to have a fourth child[24]. Similarly, findings from the 1980s showed that women in South Korea and in rural Liaoning, China, were three or four times more likely to have a third child if their first two children were daughters than if they had at least one son[25]. In South Korea at that time, women ideally wanted two sons for every daughter, just as in Punjab 20 years later. In India as a whole, demographers estimate that gender preference has the effect of raising fertility by an estimated 8 percent[26]. Thus, an effort to reduce the preference for sons could make a substantial contribution to reducing population growth.

Apart from raising general fertility levels, the link between son preference and fertility means that girls are more likely than boys to live in large families with many siblings. In the early 1990s, South Korean families with one child were more than twice as likely to have a boy as a girl (sex ratio 210), while families with five children had more than twice as many girls as boys (sex ratio 49).[27]

---

24 Arnold, Choe, and Roy, "Son Preference in India".

25 Minja Kim Choe and Seung-Kwon Kim, "Son Preference and Family Building During Fertility Transition", *Kore- Journal of Population Studies* 21, No. 1 (1998): 184-228; Minja Kim Choe, Guo Fei, Wu Jianming, and Zhang Ruyue, "Progression to Second and Third Births in China: Patterns and Covariates in Six Provinces", *International Family Planning Perspectives* 18, No. 4 (1992): 130-136.

26 R. Mutharayappa, Minja Kim Choe, Fred Arnold, and T K Roy, "Is Son Preference Slowing Down India's Transition to Low Fertility?" *NFHS Bulletin*, No. 4 (Mumbai: International Institute for Population Sciences; Honolulu: East-West Center, 1997).

27 Park and Cho, "Consequences".

Where food, healthcare and education are scarce, resources will be spread more thinly in large families with girls than in small families with boys. A village study in rural Vietnam found that, virtually all families with four or more children had only daughters. Most of these large families were living in extreme poverty[28].

If son preference plays a role in maintaining high fertility, then sex-selective abortion should contribute to fertility decline. Yet in South Korea, fertility was already declining steeply before sex-selective abortion became widely available (Figure 2), and demographic modelling suggests that, sex-selective abortion has had only a moderate effect on fertility reduction[29]. In India, fertility is much lower in the southern states of Andhra Pradesh, Karnataka, Kerala, and Tamil Nadu, where there is little evidence of sex-selective abortion, than in the northern and western states of Haryana, Punjab and Gujarat, where sex-selective abortion appears much more prevalent[30].

Figure 2: Trends in Sex Ratio at Birth and Total Fertility Rate, South Korea, 1980-2003

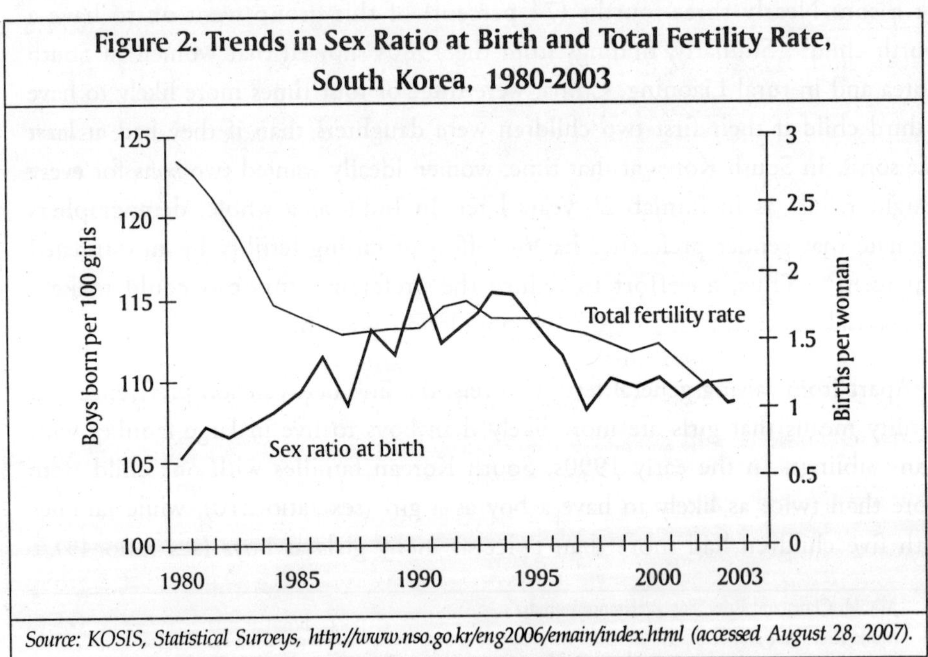

Source: KOSIS, Statistical Surveys, http://www.nso.go.kr/eng2006/emain/index.html (accessed August 28, 2007).

[28] Danièle Bélanger, "Sex-Selective Abortions: Short-term and Long-term Perspectives", *Reproductive Health Matters* 10, No. 19 (2002): 194-95.

[29] Choe and Kim, "Son Preference and Family Building".

[30] Arnold, Kishor, and Roy. "Sex-Selective Abortions in India"; International Institute for Population Sciences and ORC Macro, *National Family Health Survey (NFHS-2)*.

In a society with a strong preference for sons, couples who plan to have three children may want two sons and one daughter. But as fertility goes down, more couples may plan to have two children and they are likely to want one of each gender. Similarly, couples who only have one child, as in China, are likely to want a son, but if they have two children they may want a son and a daughter. Thus, if fertility levels converge toward the two-child family norm, the result may be a sex ratio at birth within the normal range.

Son Preference and the Marriage Market

One concern frequently voiced about son preference and the practice of sex-selective abortion is that, there will be more men than women in future adult populations. In most Asian societies, the dramatic preponderance of boys among the youngest children in large families does not have a major impact on the sex ratio of the overall population because, such large families are rare. High sex ratios for first and second births, however, may eventually affect a population's overall sex distribution.

Some observers have speculated that societies with large numbers of single young men will suffer higher crime rates and more internal unrest and violence than societies in which nearly all men "settle down" with a wife and children[31]. Similar speculation has focused on populations that experience a "youth bulge", an unusually large proportion of young adults.

A close look at social and demographic trends in China, India, and South Korea suggests that two other factors play a much more important role in the marriage market than sex-selective abortion—rapid fertility decline and the changing attitude of women toward marriage.

Rapid fertility decline: In a society with high fertility and high mortality, the population age structure resembles a pyramid, with the youngest age group at the bottom and the oldest at the top (Figure 3a). Many children are born, giving the pyramid a wide base. People die at all ages, so that, each age group is smaller than the group just younger. The result is a steadily shrinking population up to a narrow tip (the oldest age group) at the top.

[31] For example, Valerie M. Hudson and Andrea Den Boer, "A Surplus of Men, a Deficit of Peace", *International Security* 26, No. 4 (2002): 5-38.

By contrast, in a society where fertility is declining steeply or is already below replacement level (generally defined as an average of 2.1 children per woman), the "population pyramid" no longer looks like a pyramid (Figures 3b and 3c). Rather, each succeeding group of children born tends to be smaller than the group preceding it. Twenty to thirty years later, there will be fewer potential marriage partners—both men and women—at younger ages. As a result, Asian men who wish to marry younger women (and most do) will find themselves in a "marriage squeeze".

Rapid fertility decline is contributing to an unbalanced marriage market in South Korea and China. In 1990, there were 127 South Korean boys ages 5-9 years for every 100 girls ages 0-4.[32] This group of girls was the first to be affected by sex-selective abortion. But even if sex ratios at birth had been normal (i.e., if all the "missing girls" were restored), there would be 122 boys in the older age group for every 100 girls in the younger group, simply because of fertility decline. Selective abortion contributed only 4 percent to a potential "marriage squeeze".

By 2020, if a Chinese man in his late 20s is looking for a bride in her early 20s, he will be facing odds of 119 men for every 100 women. In South Korea, the odds will be even worse—at 123 men ages 25-29 for every 100 women ages 20-24. In India, the odds will be much better (at 104 men in their late 20s for every 100 women in their early 20s) because fertility was not dropping as rapidly in the 1990s. If aggregate numbers are the only thing that matters in a marriage market, then the solution for Asia's bachelors is simple: Marry an older woman. In China in 2020, for example, there will be only 97 men in their late 20s for every 100 women in their early 30s.

Women's marriage preferences: Even in societies with a relatively high percentage of women, men will have difficulty finding a bride if women choose not to marry. And if there is an expectation that a husband will have more wealth and education than his wife, then wealthy, highly educated women and poor, less-educated men will both have trouble finding spouses[33].

32 Park and Cho, "Consequences".

33 Robert D. Retherford, Naohiro Ogawa, and Rikiya Matsukura, "Late Marriage and Less Marriage in Japan", *Population and Development Review* 27, No. 1 (2001): 65-102.

Figures 3a, b, and c: Age and Sex Structure of the National Population of India, South Korea, and China, 2005

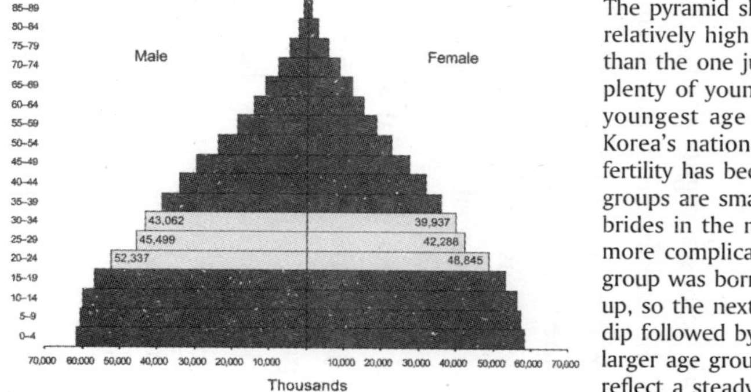

Fig. 3a. Age and sex structure of the national population of India

The pyramid shape of India's national population structure (Figure 3a) results from relatively high fertility and high mortality, with each five-year age group smaller than the one just younger, which is below. In this situation, older men should find plenty of younger women to marry. India's pyramid is less sloping for the three youngest age groups, indicating that fertility levels are coming down. South Korea's national population structure (Figure 3b) is typical of a society in which fertility has been below replacement level for some time. Most of the younger age groups are smaller than the group above. Thus older men will find fewer potential brides in the next younger age group. China's population structure (Figure 3c) is more complicated. The 45-49-year-old age group is unusually small because this group was born during the famine years of 1959-61. After the famine, fertility went up, so the next younger age groups are considerably larger. Twenty years later, this dip followed by a rise in population numbers is "echoed" as these smaller and then larger age groups had children. The small age groups at the bottom of the pyramid reflect a steady fertility decline since the early 1990s. In China, as in South Korea, a man looking for a younger wife will have relatively few women to choose from.

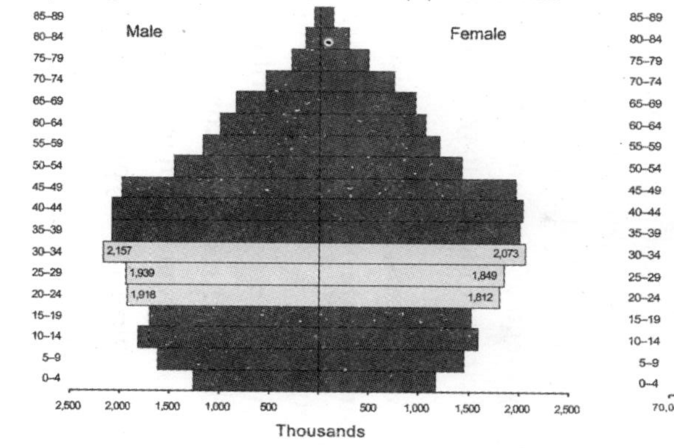

Fig. 3b. Age and sex structure of the national population of South Korea

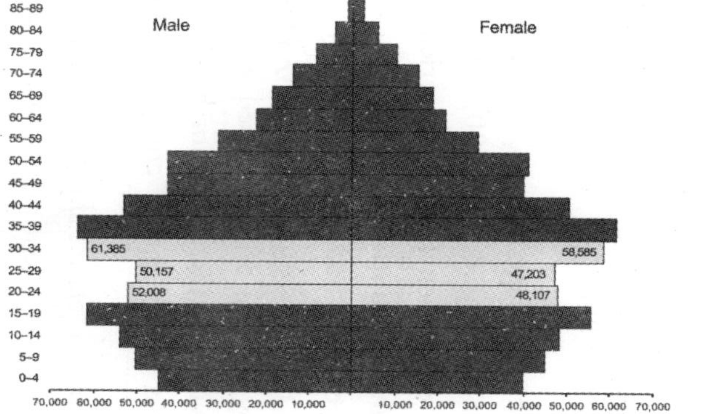

Fig. 3c. Age and sex structure of the national population of China

Source: United Nations Population Division, World Population Prospects: The 2006 Revision, Population Database, http://esa.un.org/unpp/index.asp?panel=2 (India, South Korea, and China; accessed March 20, 2007).

This appears to be happening in Japan, a country with no history of excessive female mortality or sex-selective abortion. In 2000, 8 percent of Japanese men and 9 percent of Japanese women with a university education had never married by age 50.[34] By contrast, among Japanese with junior-high-school or less education, 21 percent of men had not married by age 50, compared with 6 percent of women.

Although marriage rates are much higher in South Korea and China, a similar pattern has emerged. In 2000, among South Korean university graduates, 4 percent of women had not married by age 50, compared with 1 percent of men[35]. Among South Koreans with a junior-high-school or less education, 3 percent of men had not married by the age 50, compared with 1 percent of women. Among Chinese university graduates, 1.2 percent of women had not married by the age 50, compared with 0.4 percent of men. By contrast, among Chinese with less than a junior-high-school education, 6.8 percent of men had not married by the age 50 compared with only 0.1 percent of women.

Apart from a relative shortage of "appropriate" spouses, highly educated women have reasons to be skeptical about marriage. If they are forced to quit their jobs—which are likely to be relatively high paying—when they marry or have children, they will lose much of the investment they made in all those years of schooling, even if they eventually return to the labour force. Thus, single women who work and earn their own income may not have a strong financial incentive to marry.

Along with financial disincentives, several changes in social attitudes have made women more reluctant to marry. In Japan and South Korea, women increasingly enjoy a single lifestyle without pressure to marry. Many live with their parents and make little contribution to household expenses, leaving them with considerable disposable income. At the same time, premarital sex has become widespread. And women with married friends cannot help but notice that Japanese and South Korean men typically provide very little help with childrearing or household chores.

---

34 Robert D. Retherford and Naohiro Ogawa, *Japan's Baby Bust: Causes, Implications, and Policy Responses*, East-West Center Working Papers, Population and Health Series, No. 118 (Honolulu: East-West Center, April 2005). Also online at *http://www.eastwestcenter.org/*

35 Minja Kim Choe, "Modernization, Gender Roles and Marriage Behavior in South Korea", in *Transformations in Twentieth Century Korea*, eds. Yun-Shik Chang and Steven Hugh Lee (London: Routledge, 2006): 291-309.

Policy Response

At best, researchers can only speculate what an imbalanced sex ratio will mean for the economic, social, and political situation in South Korea, China and the northern and western states of India. These societies will have a preponderance of males in the young-adult age group, at least for a while, but this will be within populations increasingly dominated by the middle-aged and the elderly.

South Korean demographers Chai Bin Park and Nam Hoon Cho point out some effects of sex-selective abortion that might be considered positive[36]. One is a reduction in the number of unwanted children. If families want boys so badly that they impoverish themselves by having large families or let girls die through neglect or mistreatment, then perhaps it is better for them to have boys. And if the "marriage squeeze" forces men to marry older women, there should be fewer single—possibly lonely—people in old age. In India, a shortage of women could reduce the demand for dowries[37].

Looking at swings in China's marriage market due to changing birth and death rates before, during and after the 1959-61 famine, economist Maria Porter identifies some positive outcomes from periods when women were relatively scarce. She finds that women who married at a time when women were scarce tended to make "better matches" and to have more influence within the family. Further, Porter finds that children in such families were better nourished than children born to couples who married at a time when women were more abundant[38].

Regardless of long-term trends, the combination of strong son preference with modern technology poses a social, economic, and ethical dilemma for policy-makers. In South Korea, the use of foetal-screening technologies for sex-identification was outlawed in 1987. In 1990, the Korean Ministry of Health and Social Affairs increased the penalties for doctors convicted of performing the tests and suspended the medical licenses of eight physicians, an action that was widely reported in the media. In 1994, the medical code was further strengthened: Physicians who

---

36 Park and Cho, "Consequences".

37 T.V. Sekher, personal communication.

38 Maria Porter, "Imbalance in China's Marriage Market and its Effect on Intra-Household Resource Allocation", *http://home.uchicago.edu/~mporter/china_apr2007.pdf* (accessed May 7, 2007; page no longer available).

perform such tests may now be imprisoned for up to one year, may be fined up to $12,000, and may lose their medical licenses.

In May 1989, the Chinese Ministry of Health issued "An Urgent Notice on Strictly Forbidding the Use of Medical Technology to Perform Prenatal Sex Determination", which re-emphasized previous regulations. In January 2007, the Chinese government announced a crackdown on providers who perform abortions for non-medical reasons, as well as increased protections for baby girls. A statement issued jointly by the ruling Communist Party and the State Council said that people who "conduct illegal gender testing of foetuses and sex-selective abortions should face serious punishment", along with anyone who kills, abandons, or injures a baby girl[39].

In 1983, the Indian government banned sex screening in government hospitals, and in 1994 the Indian Parliament passed the Pre-natal Diagnostic Techniques Regulations and Prevention of Misuse Act, banning all fetal screening except to detect genetic abnormalities in the case of high-risk pregnancies. The Indian law requires the registration of all ultrasound machines and bans doctors from revealing the sex of the fetus to expectant parents. In March 2006, a doctor received a three-year prison sentence for telling an undercover investigator that her fetus was female and hinting that she could have an abortion[40].

These stipulations are difficult to enforce, however and the laws in these countries do not appear to have had much effect on the practice of sex-selective abortion. Some observers believe that harsh regulations have only made sex-determination procedures more clandestine and more expensive.

Many argue that the stress needs to be on addressing the attitudes of male dominance and son preference that underlie excessive female mortality and sex-selective abortion. Demographer and China specialist Judith Banister has pointed out: "In trying to counteract discrimination against female foetuses and children, (we must) emphasize not only the future dearth of available wives, but also the

39 Associated Press, "China Vows to Stop Bias Toward Male Children", *MSNBC.com*, January 22, 2007, *http://www.msnbc.msn.com/id/16750910* (accessed May 7, 2007).

40 Carla Power, "NS Special Report:...But What If It's a Girl?" *New Statesman*, April 24, 2006.

negative impacts of sex-selective abortion, female infanticide, and selective neglect of girls on today's women and girls"[41].

The problem is that, son preference is both deeply-rooted in tradition and supported by many aspects of modernization. As journalist Carla Power has observed, "For many activists, India's female foeticide problem is entwined with the consumer society the country has become over the past 15 years. If one can order a BMW, goes the mindset, one can order a boy"[42].

Both the Chinese and Indian governments are working to change this attitude. In China, the government conducts media campaigns emphasizing the value of daughters. A national program provides educational, medical, and employment benefits to families with one or two daughters and no sons[43]. And in an effort to counter the requirement for sons to provide old-age support, the Chinese government recently began paying a small allowance to rural parents age 60 and older who have no living children, only one child, or two daughters[44].

In 2003, the Indian government launched a program to help homeless women support their newborn babies with cash allowances that are twice as high for girls as for boys[45]. And recently, the Directorate of Family Welfare in Delhi launched a public-information campaign encouraging families to value daughters, with slogans such as: "Indira Gandhi and Mother Teresa: Your daughter can be one of them".

Such programs differ sharply from South Korea's slow, reluctant shift from policies that actively supported male dominance. Even today, the South Korean government does not provide financial incentives or conduct media campaigns to strengthen the position of women and girls.

---

41 Judith Banister, *Son Preference in Asia—Report of a Symposium*, United States Census Bureau, *http://www.census.gov/ipc/www/ebspr96a.html* (accessed March 15, 2007).

42 Power, "NS Special Report".

43 Zeng Yi, "Options for Fertility Policy Transition in China", *Population and Development Review* 33, No. 2 (2007): 215-46.

44 Xinhua, "Subsidy to Cover More Aged Rural Parents," on the website of National Population and Family Planning Commission of China, February 11, 2007, *http://www.npfpc.gov.cn/en/en2007-03/news20070306.htm* (accessed July 9, 2007).

45 Power, "NS Special Report".

This contrast suggests that China and India may achieve more balanced birth rates and better survival statistics for girls well before they reach the high level of economic development that South Korea currently enjoys. If their policies are successful, Asia's two most populous countries may be able to improve the lives of millions of women and girls and limit the extent of gender imbalance in their populations.

Note: The East-West Center is an education and research organization established by the US Congress in 1960 to strengthen relations and understanding among the peoples and nations of Asia, the Pacific, and the United States. The Center contributes to a peaceful, prosperous, and just Asia Pacific community by serving as a vigorous hub for cooperative research, education, and dialogue on critical issues of common concern to the Asia Pacific region and the United States. Funding for the Center comes from the US government, with additional support provided by private agencies, individuals, foundations, corporations and the governments of the region. Papers in the AsiaPacific Issues series feature topics of broad interest and significant impact relevant to current and emerging policy debates. The views expressed are those of the author and not necessarily those of the Center.

(Sidney B Westley (B.A. Smith College) is a Communications Specialist with the Research Program at the East-West Center. Ms. Westley has worked as a writer, editor and communications director for international research organizations in Ethiopia, Kenya, and the United States. She has taught courses in science writing for researchers and in science reporting for journalists. She can be reached at WestleyS@EastWestCenter.org; and

Minja Kim Choe (Ph.D. University of Hawai'i, Manoa) is a Senior Fellow in Population and Health Studies at the East-West Center. Dr. Choe's research focuses on South Korea, Japan, other Asian countries, and the United States. Her interests include family and gender issues, health behavior of adolescents and young adults, fertility and reproductive health, child survival, and statistical analysis of demographic processes. She can be reached at ChoeM@EastWestCenter.org).

7

Interventions to Balance Sex Ratio at Birth in Rural China

Zheng, Zhenzhen

Prevalent since two thousand years in China, ideal sex composition of children for most couples in China was to have one boy and one girl. Sex Ratio at Birth (SRB) has been rising since the 1980s and this boy preference has been raising a serious, common concern which needs to be dealt urgently. The imbalanced SRB is quite real but the issue is not that simple as preference for a boy is a traditional and conscious choice of parents. These traditional changes are quite slow compared to social and economic development. The higher SRB is a consequence of combined social problems caused by multiple factors and need to be resolved in a comprehensive way by the combined efforts of all sectors. Being a complicated social issue, these cannot be solved only by administrative measures. The article highlights two main strategies in balancing the SRB—one is to strictly prohibit identification of foetal sex for non-medical purposes and sex selective abortions while second is a nationwide campaign on 'Care for Girls'.

Source: www.cicred.org © Zheng, Zhenzhen. Reprinted with permission. The article was first presented at CEPED-CICRED-INED Seminar on Female Deficit in Asia: Trends and Perspectives, Singapore, 5-7 December 2005.

Background

Almost all parents have preference to the number and sex of children, somebody like boy more and somebody like girl more. The ideal sex-composition of children to most couples in China is to have one boy and one girl (Zheng, 2004), which was also true in China for the last two thousand years. If there were no limit to number of children and if a couple had very strong sex preference of children, they would give birth one after another until they achieve the ideal sex-structure of their children. However, there is hardly such a case in modern days since the higher cost of an "extra" child is not affordable to most families, the costs include economic, social, opportunity and political. A couple under the double pressure of strong sex-preference and limited number of children affordable may choose to select sex of a foetus in an unnatural way if there is a way, that is the situation in some part of China today and in some other Asian countries such as India.

The sex ratio at birth (SRB) has been rising since late 1980s in some rural areas. Existing researches and investigations show that the direct causes of higher SRB are under-reporting or misreporting of newborn girls and sex-selected induced abortion, as well as some infant abandonment and occasionally infanticide. Numerous researches have been published in the last decade on boy preference in rural China. Although the state and local government have taken specific measures such as education and prohibition of sex-selection screening and induced abortion in higher trimester, the rising SRB has been worse in some areas. In spite of the debate on the degree of seriousness, the higher SRB in most areas has raised common concern. The continuous abnormally high SRB (or, reported SRB) is a fact and need to be dealt with urgently.

Discrimination to girl is not a new issue in China. There was a higher girl infant mortality in history and the discrimination could be observed from the first two censuses in China during the early 1950s and the early 1960s (see Figure 1). While the sex ratio of infant was quite balanced in each census, it increased with age in 1953 census population, implies a consistent girl discrimination which caused a higher girl child mortality. In 1964 census, the situation improved a little. The imbalanced sex ratio at age 0 has been observed since the late 1980s. The 2000 National Census shows a strong discrimination toward female foetus rather than girl child.

Figure 1: Sex Ratio of Age 0-10 Population, 1953, 1964 and 2000

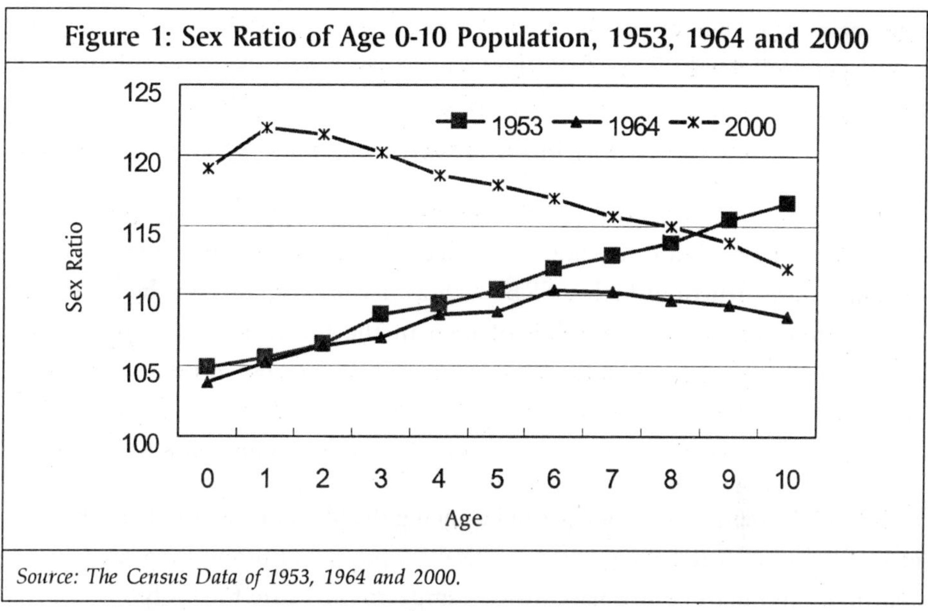

Source: The Census Data of 1953, 1964 and 2000.

The imbalanced SRB was believed a consequence of under-report or misreport of girl child and sex selected induced abortion mainly in the 1990s (Zeng, *et. al.*,, 1993), however, it is found that even more boys were under-reported during the 2000 Census, which tells that the imbalanced SRB is quite real (Yu, 2003). Although son preference is the first reason to be blamed, the issue is not that simple. Preference for boy and discrimination to girl has a long tradition in China, which is a bad tradition indeed. However, such a preference is also a conscious choice of parents. Preference to boy is related to traditional family role of boy and girl, such a tradition changes very slow compared to social and economic development. The gender role in most societies also favour male and not female. Although women's rights and benefits has always been protected by written laws and regulations, they are often violated and neglected in practice. Women were found often in disadvantaged position in education, employment, promotion, marriage, family responsibility, land distribution, and in heritage. The national principle of "men and women are equal" remains an abstract slogan in some occasions, and negatively impacted women's status and development. The parents are well aware of the inequity of men and women and hence, expect that a son would have better future and therefore, a higher payback. Furthermore, the traditional responsibility of old age care is taken by son and daughter-in-law in most parts of China, especially in rural areas, where family support is almost the sole depend of elderly. Therefore, the higher SRB is a consequence of combined social problems and caused by multiple factors, the problem is a need to be solved in a comprehensive way by all sectors' combined efforts.

The response to imbalanced SRB published by 2000 National Census seem to miss the mark, most discussions in media even in academic field focuses on the possible consequences of higher SRB, such as marriage squeeze in the future and even with a certain large number of men in the future may not find a wife. Furthermore, the responsibility of balancing the SRB seems to be on population and family planning sectors and the department responsible to the job is IEC under the National Population and Family Planning Commission.

There are mainly two strategies in balancing the SRB, one is strictly prohibiting identification of foetal sex for non-medical purposes and prohibiting sex-selective abortions, another one is a nationwide campaign on "Care for Girls".

The imbalanced sex ratio at birth is a complicated social issue and it could not be solved only by administrative measures. The changes to a more favourable social economic environment, changes in people's mind and practice also need to happen simultaneously. Hence, there is a great and urgent need to review and assess existing intervention measures, study and develop more specific, more comprehensive and more effective intervention strategies.

This paper will review the current measures to balancing the high SRB, and discuss possible.

Research Framework

According to the existing research results, the direct causes of a higher SRB may be: (1) son preference of couples; (2) easily accessible methods of foetus sex identification; and (3) medical or family planning service capable on higher trimester induced abortion. The most popular method for foetus sex identification is the use of ultrasonic device, such a device is widely available in public and private clinics of every county in China, both urban and rural people can easily have the service with an affordable amount of cost. For example, some news reported that the cost for foetus sex-identification is only 50 RMB yuan in Guangdong rural area. According to the family planning technical service protocol of China, only hospitals or family planning service stations at county level or higher are certified for higher trimester pregnancy termination, for medical reasons. However, the implementation of the protocol and the management of pregnancy termination for non-medical reasons are relatively poor in some areas, which made possible sex-selective induced abortions. Although, the government has a strong desire to control the practice of foetus sex-identification and sex-selective induced abortion, couple's desire to have a son is even stronger in some areas. The son preference is affected by other factors combined together, such as local traditions, social-economic status, related policies, *et. al.*

Figure 2 is a research framework about the determinants of higher SRB. This article will be structured as the framework, to investigate each factor and discuss the current measures taken and possibility of further intervention. There are six parts in the figure, say, social environment, economic development, family needs, individual opinion, administrative strength and technical capability. The six parts not only play independent roles in SRB, but also are interconnected with each other, and the independent variables as well as their interactions affect the outcome variable in our study, the sex ratio at birth. The last two sets of factors, administrative/management factors and technical factors are actually the intervention measure at the end of line and they are the parts that most intervention actions take place in China, they will not be the focus of this article.

Social Environment

Women's rights and benefits are all well-defined in related national laws and policies; however, the enforcement of those laws and policies still need to be monitored to ensure the rights and benefits. Some experts suggested that the existing laws and policies need to be improved for gender equity; for example, the legal retirement age for government employee is 60 for men and 55 for women. Some local policies intend to favour families with only girls (mostly in land distribution), but still some other policies are not.

Although educational attainment for women has been improved in the last several decades, women's average year of education is still less than that of men (Zheng and Lian, 2004), which is one result of lower economic status and lower political participation of women.

Figure 2: An Analytic Framework of SRB Determinants

Determinant	Factors	
Social environment	Traditional practice of marriage The role of media Women's economic and family status Policies that do not protect women's rights	
Economic development	Local economic development status Support system for the elderly Migration of labour force Women's employment	
Family needs	Function and role of children Old age support Land distribution practice Family need of labour	Sex ratio at birth
Individual opinion	Son dependence of old age care Continuing of family line Preference of boy	
Administrative management	Government's attention to deal with SRB Management of B scan equipment Management to higher trimester induced abortion	
Technical capability	Awareness to SRB among technical service providers Technical capacity of local public service Technical capacity of private sectors	

It is also found that there is a wage difference between female and male workers. The wage gap due to the difference in sector occupation is small; most of the wage difference between females and males is caused by discrimination, especially among the less prestigious occupations (Zhang, 2004). Empirical research also found that the threshold for women to enter labour market is higher than that of men and women exit (retire) from formal employment earlier than men (Cai, 2002, pp245-286).

Tradition role of women in family and the marriage custom also put women in a disadvantaged position. In most places of rural China, wife lives with the family of her husband and women is only responsible to household works within the family. The traditional practice does not encourage parents to invest much on a girl's education since she is going to be married out to other family and women is less likely to participate in village public affairs. In some counties of Hubei Province where son preference is not strong, there is a tradition of husband living with wife's family and daughter is responsible to take care of the elderly. It is found that, SRB had been always normal in these areas.

The public image of women is also often stereotyped by media and in textbooks. Women are often portrayed as a good wife or in a vulnerable position to be protected. The way that media addresses the problem of imbalanced sex-ratio is to assume the shortage of women or shortage of potential wives for men. Such comments and assumptions are somehow misleading the public (Bu, 2004).

Economic Development

Researches found that the relationship between SRB and economic development are mixed and complicated. A higher SRB was observed in the eastern coastal area in China around late 1980s and early 1990s, but not necessarily universal. For example, Zhejiang Province had a relatively higher SRB in 1990 Census, but three counties inside Zhejiang kept a quite balanced SRB. The situation has been improving during the last decade in most parts of Zhejiang, given the economy there is still growing.

According to the data provided by 2000 National Census, sex ratios at birth are higher in eastern and southern China and it is found not correlated with economic factors at provincial level (Wang and Huang, 2004).

Economic development was to found to affect son-preference in different ways: (1) a community with a better economic situation is able to set up old age security/ support system so, local people do not expect to depend on the son providing support when they become older; (2) a developed local economy increases local employment, especially some labour intensive enterprises prefer to recruit young women workers, which increased the proportion of rural women who work in a paid job and sometimes, lead to an improvement in women's status inside and outside the family; (3) family with more income could afford to seek sex-identification techniques so, sex-selected induced abortion could be more popular; (4) where private business is booming, a rich family desperately needs a son to take over the family business.

It is commonly agreed that economic development does not solve the problem of SRB imbalance naturally, but may play an indirect positive role.

Labor force migration is another social/demographic change that could have positive effect on SRB balance. The migration from rural to urban may change the opinion of rural couples and assimilate rural people, especially youth, with urban life styles, including the fertility desire (You and Zheng, 2002), therefore weaken the son-preference. Migration also creates an opportunity for rural women to work and earn salary, which in turns re-value the role of woman in a family. A study that took place in the rural areas of Sichuan and Anhui in 2000 found that comparing to women who never migrated, returned migrant women were more open-minded about gender relationships and more confident in negotiating with husbands; they hold a less "traditional" attitude toward the husband/wife relationship, have more knowledge and awareness about reproductive health and tend to desire late marriage and fewer children. The research found that migration experience has served as catalyst to have a positive and pronounced impact on women's empowerment, sometimes directly and sometimes through the increased income that women's migration brings to the rural family. Many of the quantitative findings of the study have shown that the effect of migration is significant when other variables are controlled (Zheng and Gu, 2004).

Family Needs

As mentioned earlier, the need for a son is often a conscious decision of couples, after balancing the cost and benefit of children in their life. Since the role of children in a family is often clearly defined, preference of a son is quite reasonable for those who still depend on son(s) to provide support in old age, to work in a farm or in a family business, to deal with family affairs, and carry on the family name (Xie, 2002). Although agricultural modernization is on the way, in some rural area a son or sons are still needed for heavy labour, for example, in less developed mountainous areas.

Numerous journal articles and discussions emphasize the importance of a son to a family: son(s) as the key for old age support, as the head of the family, as an honour of the family and as one kind of goods that every family has. Son-preference is also related to a family's status. It is found that couples are more desperate in need of a son if the family has lower social status in the village. As the management on controlling of sex-selective abortion is often put burden on the pregnant woman, woman are in double jeopardy—subjects of controlling the sex-selective induced abortion and pressure to give a male birth within a family. In some rural area, a woman could be divorced if she could not give birth to a son.

An anthropological study in Zhejiang village explained that the family needs often were put on the top of individual's need among rural residents (Li and Chen, 1993). The deeply rooted family need and culture regarding to roles of son and daughter are very difficult to be removed in a short period of time; they would be far behind any social and economic development. By reviewing all surveys about fertility desire, one of the conclusions is that, the desire for a number of children has been changed during the last two decades, but the preference for the sex composition of children has not changed too much (Feng and Zhang, 2002).

Some of the needs of sons could be simply blamed as an old tradition, but some of the needs are quite practical and reasonable. Unless the society and the government solve the problems of old age support and to reform the agriculture structure, some needs of sons will sustain regardless all the campaigns and IEC activities.

Interventions to Balance Sex Ratio at Birth

The serious imbalanced sex ratio at birth has raised concern of the Chinese government. The national leader Hu Jintao emphasized the importance of a normal SRB and suggested a goal to stop the rising SRB in the next three to five years. The issue is also included in the "Suggestions to Develop the 11th Five Year Plan for Economic and Social Development" by the Central Committee of CCP

(The 5th Meeting of 16th CCP, 2005), which identifies that bringing SRB back to normal range as one of the major tasks in the next five years.

(1) Legal Intervention

In fact, the issue had raised attention of the government back to late 1980s. Ministry of Health and State Family Planning Commission jointly distributed a regulation by Beijing Family Planning Commission and Bureau of Health on "Prohibition of foetus sex identification for non-medical purposes" in 1986. Ministry of Health distributed an urgent notice on "Strictly prohibition of medical practice on foetus sex-identification and abuse of techniques of artificial insemination" in 1989. Another joint notice issued by the Ministry of Health and the State Family Planning Commission was distributed in 1993 on "Restatement on the prohibition of foetus sex-identification practice". The Supreme Court and the Supreme Procuratorate issued a notice on "Punishment according to the law on criminals against family planning". Law of Maternal and Child Health implemented in 1995 is the first law states that foetus sex-identification is strictly prohibited.

Article 22 in the Law of Population and Family Planning states that "Discrimination against and maltreatment of women who give births to baby girls or who suffer from infertility are prohibited. Discrimination against, maltreatment, and abandonment of baby girls are prohibited". Article 35 in the law again states that the "Use of ultrasonography or other techniques to identify gender of foetus for non-medical purposes is strictly prohibited. Sex-selective pregnancy termination for non-medical purposes is strictly prohibited".

In the year 2002, National Population and Family Planning Commission, Ministry of Health, and State Food and Drug Administration jointly issued a "Regulation of Prohibition of Foetus Sex Identification and Sex Selective Pregnancy Termination for Non-Medical Reasons (referred as the Prohibition Regulation later in this report)."

In 1998 and 2002, National Population and Family Planning Commission jointly issued documents to intervene imbalanced SRB comprehensively with other 11 ministries. The documents defined responsibilities of each ministry/sectors to keep the SRB at normal level.

There are mainly five legal ways to stop foetus sex-identification and sex-selective induced abortion.

1) Definition of legal foetus sex-identification practice.

   As defined by the laws (Maternal and Child Health, Population and Family Planning), foetus sex-identification and sex-selective induced abortion for non-medical purposes are illegal, and any violation of the law will subject to criminal sanction and confiscation of license.

2) Prohibition of sex-selective pregnancy termination.

   The punishments for non-medical purpose of sex selective pregnancy termination are: confiscating earnings from services, fine, licence cancellation, and even criminal sanction.

3) Control the distribution of abortion pills.

   Abortion pills should only be available at certified health and family planning institutions and should not be sold in any retail drugstore or by any individual.

4) Infant death report system

   Medical institutions should provide death certificate for newborn deaths in the institution and inform local family planning department about the event. Parents should report newborn death within 48 hours to local government and family planning department, if the death happens outside medical institution. Any practice of making fake death certification is criminal.

Amendment of Law of Protection on Women's Right and Benefit (took place in 2005) should be helpful in solving the problem of son preference in an indirect way. Changes in other Laws and regulations even take longer time, but some laws and regulations in the process of initiation and modification have considered gender equity issues, such as the draft of Labor and Employment Law stated that sex discrimination in employment is illegal.

(2) "Care for Girls" Campaign

The National Population and Family Planning started a pilot intervention project, Care for Girls, in March 2003. The short-term goal of the project is to create a favourable environment nationwide for girls' development and reverse the trend of increasing high SRB through integrated measures in the next three to five years. The long-term goals are: (1) to create an incentive mechanism nationwide for girls' development and for families practised birth control with only female children; (2) to change the fertility ideology of public regarding sex preference; and (3) to balance SRB by year of 2010 (NPFPC, 2005). The project has been implemented in 11 provinces with most serious high level of SRB, and one county with highest SRB was selected as pilot county in each province. The project activities including advocacy and publicity through media and other IEC approaches, to help girls stay in school and complete nine-year education, to help the families in poverty with only daughters, and to encourage newly married couples reverse the tradition of living arrangement. The project also emphasizes on administrative measures to crack down on foetal sex identification practices and sex-selective induced abortion and to eliminate female infanticide or girl baby abandonment. However, the effect of such a campaign has never been formally assessed, and tradition may not change in such a short time.

(3) Other Related Activities

There are other governmental activities that played a role to balance the SRB, though not initiated for the purpose.

The Publicity Department of CCP and NPFPC initiated a campaign in early 1999 called **"new notion of marriage and childbearing into ten thousand families"**, and the campaign will continue for the next five years. This campaign aims at changing the traditional customs on marriage and childbearing. The slogans of the campaign include "men and women should be equal", "sons and daughters are both blessings to the family", "daughter should also carry on the family name", "husband should be responsible to family planning". Gradually the campaign integrated with "Care for Girls" IEC activities.

The **Program of Happiness**, a project especially set up to help impoverished mothers, has helped them to improve their life quality, not only lending them money but also paving the way to self-support. Launched a decade ago in Beijing by non-profit organizations, China Population Welfare Foundation, the China Family Planning Association and the *China Population Daily*, the program has funded about 150,000 impoverished mothers with an accumulative 260 million yuan (US$32.1 million) in 341 counties throughout the country by the end of 2004. As a result, some 600,000 people have benefited from the program.

Another program piloted in the year 2004 in some mid-western rural areas to support only child or two-daughter families by a subsidy of 600 RMB Yuan annually to each parent who is 60 or older through the rest of their life. It is called "The System of Social Support for Some Rural Families Practicing Family Planning (**Social Support System**)". This system is an incentive or reward to those who practised family planning according to the local family planning regulations. Although the amount of money is not very large, it is still useful for the elderly in the less developed rural areas. It also serves as a message of government support, especially to couples who do not have a son. At the same time, the central government encouraged the eastern provinces to initiate local pilot programs of social support with their own fund. In the state-designated and locally initiated pilot sites, this system has benefited 310,000 and 500,000 rural residents respectively, involving a total of 1.8 million people in families that practiced birth control (Pan, 2005).

(4) Administrative Management

All provinces/autonomous region/municipalities have defined administrative review and approve procedure for induced abortion beyond 14-16 weeks of pregnancy and all regulations modified according to the Law of Population and Family Planning also have defined that the practice of fetus sex identification and sex selective induced abortion are illegal. Some provincial regulations have detailed definition and punishment to any violation. For example, the Regulation of Family Planning of Hebei Province states that couples had induced abortion beyond 14 weeks of the pregnancy (second parity) without approve by county family planning department cannot get official approval for another pregnancy.

Regulations also applied to the operation of ultra-sound scan machine. For example, it required that two technicians should be present at the time of use of ultra-sound machines for maternal check-up, to prevent any possible sex-identification practice of individuals.

Up to date, the campaign against discrimination to female foetus and to baby girls have mainly been implemented by National Population and Family Planning Commission as well as All China Women's Federation, there is still need a joint force from other governmental departments and from civil society organizations. Furthermore, the participation of local people is very important to the intervention, it will strengthen the positive effect.

Discussion: Intervention in Combined Effort and with a Clear Target

The ongoing interventions, if well-designed and implemented, will have some short- and long-term effects. The prohibition of foetal sex identification would have stopped the practice temporarily, but the effectiveness in the long-run is questionable, if the causes of girl discrimination were not eliminated. Some local regulation eliminate induced abortion in higher trimester to only medical need, which may force such a practice go underground, and make the practice more harmful to the women. Meanwhile, study and formulate socio-economic policies and social security systems favourable for girls' growth and for families with only female children would be more effective in the long-run, but, the process needs time. Any expectation on immediate impact is not practical. If the main efforts were put on the short-term effect intervention, more opportunity and more time will be lost.

Not all couples in childbearing age have an intension to select the sex of foetus, the practice is quite limited and has clear local patterns. The right target group need to be identified to work with. The pilot program of "Care for Girls" has been carried out in 11 county/cities where the SRB at 2000 was found more higher, this could be seen as a way of targeting. On the other side, the opinion and need of target group should also be identified to design specific interventions. Up to date there is no publication mentioned any needs assessment in a standard way. None of the pilot program has been assessed on the impact yet.

The interventions or activities/programs that were not initiated for the purpose but have a significant contribution, can be classified into three categories: incentives, advocacy, and legal/administrative management. Based on results from a research supported by China/UNFPA country project (2005), the characteristics of and comments for the three approaches are summarized in Table 1.

Table 1: A Summary of Current Interventions on High SRB

Activity/program	Target Population	Long-Term Effect	Short-Term Effect	Comments
Social support system	Rural parents ≥ age 60 with 1 child or 2 daughters	Encouraging	Unclear yet	Need to convince people that it is not a temporary policy
Family planning incentive regulation or activities	One-child or two-daughter families and the children	Encouraging	Some effects observed	Some incentives depend on local government finance
Advocacy campaign/IEC	Couples of childbearing age and all people	Encouraging	Observable effect	Should develop advocacy strategy targeting leaders
Management of foetus sex identification	Couples who are eager or curious to know the sex of foetus	?	Somewhat effective	Need awareness and full co-operation of public and private sectors as well as effective strategies
Management of sex selective induced abortion	Couples with strong desire to have a son	?	Somewhat effective	Difficult in full control; may lead to some ethical problems

Advocacy is necessary and somewhat effective but the targeting population should be redefined or adjusted. Legal/administrative management intervention may have an immediate effect but need to be reviewed and assessed from different perspectives. Incentive/social support programs should be strongly recommended for achieving a long-term effect.

(Zheng, Zhenzhen, Institute of Population and Labor Economics Chinese Academy of Social Sciences Beijing, China.)

References

1. Bu Wei. A issue of bachelor or girl's human rights?. Paper presented in the Expert Workshop on Sex Ratio Imbalance (0-4 years), Beijing, June 2004.
2. Cai Fang edt. Employment in Rural and Urban China: Issues and Options. Social Sciences Documentation Publishing House, 2002.
3. Feng Xiaotian and Zhang Qingsong. Fertility Desire Change over 20 Years in Rural and Urban. Market and Demographic Analysis, 2002(5): 21-23.
4. Li Yinhe, Chen Junjie. Individual, Family, and Childbearing Opinions. *Sociological Research*, 1993(2).

5. National Population and Family Planning Commission (NPFPC). Piloting the Care for Girls Program. *China Population Today*. August, 2005(3-4).
6. Wang Yan and Huang Mei. Study of Sex Ratio at Birth in China. Research Report (un-published), 2004.
7. Xie Zhenming. Three Key Determinants of SRB in China. *Population Research*, 2002(5).
8. You Danzhen, Zheng Zhenzhen. Fertility Desire of Returned Migrants in Rural China. *Sociological Research*, 2002(6): 52-62.
9. Yu Hongwen. The higher SRB: a miss enumeration or a fact. *Population Research*, 2003(5).
10. Zeng Yi; Tu Ping; Gu Baochang; Xu Yi; Li Bohua; Li Yongping. Causes and Implication of the Recent Increase in the Reported Sex Ratio at Birth in China. *Population and Development Review*, Vol.19, No.2 (June, 1993), 283-302.
11. Zhang Dandan. Marketization and Gender Wage Differentials. *Chinese Journal of Population Science*, 2004(1): 32-41.
12. Zheng Zhenzhen. Fertility Desire of Married Women in China. *Chinese Journal of Population Science*, 2004(5): 73-78.
13. Zheng Zhenzhen and Gu Baochang. Migration experience and women's empowerment in China. In: ICPD+10: in China, 2004.
14. Zheng Zhenzhen and Lian Pengling. Gender Differences in Education among Chinese Population. *Collection of Women's Studies*, 2004(5): 14-18.
15. Pan Guiyu. Speech at the Press Conference on the Launch of Social Support System. June 2005. (*http://www.npfpc.gov.cn/en/en2005-06/enews20050614-1.htm*).

Will Men have Difficulty in Finding a Wife in Urban China?

– Meenu Bhatnagar

Most of the countries in the Asian region are bound by the traditional and cultural elements of preference for sons. The government interventions, rules, regulations have not been able to change the mindset of people showing preference for sons over daughters. The role and cost of technology in unbalancing the gender ratio are apparent in countries like China. China's one child policy was introduced with the purpose of controlling the population but many complex issues evolved, leading to a growing gender gap in favour of boys.

Highly imbalanced sex ratios resulted in unforeseen difficulties. China's 'one-child policy' prevented more than 400 million births spread over three decades. The worst gender imbalance thus created has hit the important resource of cheap labour. It has forced millions of men to a life of loneliness. These men of marriageable age are a problem for the government and for the society at large. The safety of women is at risk at the hands of these unmarried men. Due to female infanticide and sex-selective abortions, the excess males born would find it very tough to find wives for themselves.

Human trafficking is on the increase as unmarried men are going out of their way to find wives for themselves by purchasing them, bringing wives from other countries etc. Just as the effect of one-child policy took years to unfold which lead to gender imbalance, it would take years to correct the gender ratio imbalance in the near future. Meanwhile, what would happen to large gender imbalance which is looming large? Where would the wives for these men come from? The mixing of cultures and traditions of other countries in such marriages would give rise to other problems.

Affluent urban China may be able to bring wives from other countries but what would happen to the local marriage market. The issue of gender imbalance cannot be resolved within the country itself. The gender imbalance would give rise to another phenomenon of ageing population and rapid urbanization resulting in a destabilized society. Prostitution would increase whereas violence against women and kidnappings would take place.

According to the latest figures, in China there are approximately 18 million more males of marriageable age than females. The ratio is much above the normal level and continues to surpass at an alarming rate. Delayed marriages by women due to education, technology advancement, career aspirations, low fertility etc., are bound to aggravate a situation. Coupled with gender ratio imbalance, social ills prevalent in our Asian culture of son preference would add to the woes of unmarried men from finding a mate for themselves in urban areas of China.

(Meenu Bhatnagar is a Faculty Associate at Icfai Research Centre, Ahmedabad, Gujarat. She can be reached at meenub@ibsindia.org).

8

The Daughter Deficit

Exploring Declining Sex Ratios in India

The census revealed that the phenomenon of sex ratio imbalance reached alarming proportions in states having no prior history or practice of female infanticide or where forms of discrimination against girls were not strongly evident earlier. The mistreatment of girls spans across the spectrum of Indian regions, economic classes and castes, due to complex mix of economic, social and cultural factors. Some of the trends like son preference, disaffection for daughters, family planning for sons, sex selection practices, causes of childhood deaths and dealing with subsequent consequences are elaborated. The article examines the factors contributing to the male/female imbalance in the selected districts of five Indian states of Madhya Pradesh, Rajasthan, Himachal Pradesh, Punjab and Haryana.

In a "normal world", the female population equals or slightly surpasses the number of males. Except in India, that is, where the situation is just the opposite, where the gender ratio—or the number of females to males—is known to be among the most imbalanced in the world. Although China has the most severe shortage of girls compared to boys of any country in the world today, in India, the 2001 census revealed disturbing news: the proportion of girls aged 0-6 years dropped from 945:1000 to 927:1000, since the previous census done 10 years earlier.

This means that, 35 million fewer females than males were registered in India over this particular decade. The census also revealed that the phenomenon has reached high proportions in states which had no prior history or practice of female infanticide or where forms of discrimination against girls were not strongly evident earlier.

A National Emergency

India's Census Commissioner Jayant Kumar Banthia's First Report on Religion Data, 2001, first revealed the persistent bias against the girl-child, prompting discussion of this dramatic trend.

Some voices, such as India's national newspaper, *The Hindu,* recognized the sharp decline as a national emergency. In its August 29, 2004 online article, "No girls please, we're Indian", reporter Kalpana Sharma wrote about sex-selective abortion, infanticide and the neglect/discrimination of India's girl child, calling it "...an epidemic that will have far-reaching social consequences". The reasons behind this mistreatment of girls crosses the spectrum of Indian regions, economic classes, and castes and are due to a complex mix of economic, social and cultural factors.

An Innovative Research Approach

While studies on the declining sex ratio have tended to be quantitative, looking at biological or demographic factors, there has been a lack of data on prevailing socio-economic and cultural aspects. For this reason, Canada's International Development Research Centre (IDRC), through its Women's Rights and Citizenship program and in partnership with the Indian non-governmental organization ActionAid India, is documenting the factors contributing to this male/female imbalance in select districts in the five states of Madhya Pradesh, Rajasthan, Himachal Pradesh, Punjab and Haryana.

The study, coordinated by ActionAid India's Gender Unit, focuses on six field sites—half urban, the other half rural—in two sites in three of the states, except in Punjab and Haryana where there were four sites per state.They were chosen to make the comparison between areas that have a longer history of adverse sex ratios with those where "masculinization" of the population is a more recent trend.

The Son-Preference Trend in Northern India

So far in Himachal Pradesh, Madhya Pradesh and Rajasthan, the researchers have looked at changes in education, employment, nutrition, work patterns, religion and culture, as well as family concerns such as marriage, property, inheritance and continuity. The chosen field varies, in terms of economic status, with Himachal Pradesh being by far the most prosperous. In comparison, Madhya Pradesh and Rajasthan are less well-off, with greater dependence on agriculture and lower levels of education and health care. Because morbidity levels are higher there, the researchers noted that adverse sex ratios could not be attributed to sex-selective abortions alone. Conclusive data analysis for Punjab and Haryana has not yet been completed.

What the researchers can state is that, sex ratios varied in villages and urban wards, underscoring that local contexts were significant. Son-preference was noted as being equally strong among different income groups and there was no significant correlation between caste and sex ratios where earlier research showed that sex ratios were better among lower castes and among the poor.

A Disaffection for Daughters

What are the reasons behind these trends? The findings confirmed norms that have been part of India's socio-economic fabric for centuries. Sons are considered pivotal to family welfare, as they are the ones who earn money, continue family lineage and provide a form of old age security for parents. A daughter, meanwhile, is considered to be a "double loss" as she not only leaves her family when she marries, becoming an "asset" to her new family, but she is also a source of marriage expenses, including the payment of dowry to the groom's family.

In both rural and urban Morena, Madhya Pradesh, residents keenly agreed with one respondent's comment that "...from the moment a daughter is born, the paramount concern of the immediate family is to accumulate money, valuables, and goods for her wedding". Today, dowry is a practice found among almost all castes, with the reported exception of some tribal groups. A Dhobi (lower caste) mother said, "Dowry is like a penalty... it's for the girl's security/prosperity, but whether she remains happy or not is decided by her destiny... ." She and others added that while parents fret about post-marriage security and their girls' happiness, they would resist them returning home after an unsuccessful marriage.

From the other "camp", an individual reacted to the idea of her new daughter-in-law remaining at work. "Why do we get daughters-in-law? So that, we get some rest and peace. If she goes out to work then I will have to do her job instead... ." The report notes that in instances where women might work—in the fields or in a family business—their contribution is often unrecorded and unacknowledged.

Family Planning – For Sons

Some new trends, such as the two-child family encouraged by the Indian government, and an emphasis on education also influence decisions. However, the study notes that although small families are accepted in Himachal Pradesh, Punjab, and Haryana, family planning effectively means, "planning for sons".

Generally, people want educated daughters-inlaw, although the researchers state it "...is oriented towards the future family of the couple—children will get proper guidance and instructions from an educated mother...marriage prospects rather than employment appear to drive education". However, parents expressed the hope that more education for girls would result in them obtaining white-collar, regular, and secure work pre-marriage—and a better choice of prospective husbands. In rural areas, there may be a compromise in the duration of schooling. It is noted "... girls are encouraged to complete as much education as they can—but—if a 'good match' is found, the girl is married off before she completes her studies".

Since the 1980s, technology widely available in India, such as amniocentesis and ultrasound, has permitted parents to predetermine the size and gender composition of their families through abortion.

Sex-Selection Practices

Many informants told the researchers that they did not stop at one abortion, but had three or four—sometimes more—because a girl had been conceived each time. "Abortion", says the report, "...is the method of family planning par excellence —to limit family size, to enable spacing between children and also to regulate the sex composition of the family".

Although sex-selective abortion is illegal in India, it is rarely prosecuted. Women who are most aware of the official position—the urban middle class—usually denied the practice of sex-selective abortions. At the same time, note the researchers, the urgency to have a son appears "...with a greater and more universal tone in the urban settings, as compared to the rural settings".

And yet, researchers noted that, members of the older generation referred to children as nature's or a divine gift and of the sin of getting rid of a child. Women of reproductive age may agree with this view and may protest, but the statistics show that they are not winning. "Our informants spoke of arguments between spouses about a daughter's birth. Women expressed a sullen resentment at repeated abortions, or sorrow at the loss of unborn daughters or sons (by mistake)".

Changes in work, education, marriage age and marriage costs also seem to add up to a disaffection for daughters, to a greater extent than before. The factors causing this include: increased investment that has to be made in daughters in terms of education and marriage; the loss of their material and labour support; fears for their sexual safety and security; and worries about their future happiness in an appropriate marriage.

Neglect of girls, whether planned or inadvertent, also contributes to the lower child sex ratio. While the researchers found that the degree of discrimination varied by location, there nonetheless was widespread evidence of lower levels of nutrition, health care, schooling, and emotional care, and high levels of underimmunization in general. "With nutrition and health, who may or may not take the decision is uncertain, but the discrimination is evident", say the researchers.

Causes of Childhood Deaths

The research has shown a higher death rate among girls in the one-month to one-year age group, especially from gastrointestinal disease, pneumonia, and "miscellaneous" causes.

Among their observations, the researchers note that the most common cause of death is fever, although less so for urban males in this category; for rural males and rural and urban females, mortality due to fever is about 40%. "Don't know" was often given as cause of death for all groups, apart from urban males but especially for urban females. The data indicates that urban males under one month of age are taken for medical care more often than rural neonates and urban girls.

Observations in Rajasthan also point to infectious diseases as a common cause of death. Accidents and stillbirths also contribute to mortality. "This brings into the picture the possibility of not merely biological, but also social causes of death, which would then affect female survival", the researchers note.

Dealing with the Consequences

Some states now experience a shortage of brides because of the adverse sex ratios. The study also notes that 20% or more men in some states, including Haryana and Punjab, may remain unmarried. There are already examples of brides being "imported" from poorer eastern states.

Trends to higher age at marriage, more so in urban settings, were also observed, possibly as a function of the emphasis on education. In urban Morena, Madhya Pradesh, an interviewee observed that the average age at marriage is now 20 for boys and 17 to 18 for girls, where earlier both were married at 14 years of age. This led the researchers to question if perhaps the rise in marriage age may be due to greater difficulty in finding an eligible spouse, with factors such as education, earning capacity, and dowries raising the stakes for the ideal match.

On the other hand, the researchers report that the idea a woman may remain unmarried is "total anathema". "All the informants made similar remarks—that even the "richest person on earth" cannot take the financial responsibility of an unmarried daughter". Also, ensuring a girl's chastity is considered a great parental responsibility and is one of the arguments for promoting early marriage.

How Research Approaches Can Effect Change

The research methodology used to collect data for this four-year project entailed much more than data collection. The study's objectives included understanding how social class, caste, community, occupation, marital status, age, and type of household factor into the current sex-ratio imbalance in India. A second objective was to develop a viable research methodology using a blend of quantitative and qualitative techniques. With the assistance of an interdisciplinary advisory team from Delhi University, the Indian Institute of Technology, and Jawaharlal Nehru University, a household census was carried out in select villages and wards in five states with adverse sex ratios. The research used a feminist methodology and a qualitative field-based study in the selected districts in five states. The selection of the case studies took into account the heterogeneities of caste, class, and community. In the ethnographic phase, the research was based on participant observation. Researchers spent several months living with families in the selected locations.

For better or worse, some of the usual social, cultural and economic norms in Indian society's choice of mates may be swayed. In some regions inter-caste marriage, marriage with girls of tribal communities and polyandry are now becoming more common. There are also reports of bride buying and forced remarriage of widows. Some suggest that in the near future social tension could rise because of the challenge of finding female partners, and may lead to crimes against women. Others wonder if a shortage of women will lead to less violence against them or a decrease in dowries.

As the researchers note, the increasing imbalance in sex ratios is a sign of continued inequality between the sexes. The scarcity of females, they add, is symptomatic of their low value.

Finding Solutions

The research team underscored there are both long-term and short-term measures to stem the declining female ratio. In the long-term, they recommend ensuring equal entitlements such as property rights, equal access to nutrition, health, education and affection and addressing the overall question of dowry and the necessity of marriage. In the short-term, incentives to educate girls, financial support for girls, educating health care professionals and stopping incentives for sterilization are suggested.

In July 2007, India's Women and Child Development Minister, Renuka Chowdhury, proposed that, all pregnant women register with the government and seek its permission if they wish to undergo an abortion, stating that this is aimed at stopping the aborting of unwanted female foetuses. However, critics warn that the new move could backfire and be misused.

The researchers offer the following conclusions and suggestions:

> *It will not be enough to counter son-preference. Aversion to daughters has to be squarely confronted through policy measures that increase the economic worth and support of daughters through improved employment opportunities and recognizing that women's health and education is tied to more than the mothering roles.*

The reports from the five regions will form the basis for local interventions by ActionAid India and other women's and community organizations.

9

Dispensable Daughters and Bachelor Sons

Sex Discrimination in North India

Ravinder Kaur

Daughters may not be wanted but daughters-in-law are necessary for family well-being and perpetuation. Similarly, not all sons in the family receive equal treatment and those who are left bachelors suffer a lesser fate. This article attempts to move beyond currently available explanations of low sex ratios and daughter elimination. While supporting the hypothesis that, large peasant castes in the north and north-west practised infanticide, non-marriage of men and polyandry as strategies to control family numbers in relation to available resources, this article makes three arguments: one, that these strategies occurred together, two, that one needs to go beyond this explanation to understand why daughters were the dispensable ones and three, that the number of sons wanted was by no means unlimited.

While pursuing the puzzle of the unwantedness of daughters, I was struck by certain parallels among contemporary northern jat and southern gounder peasant households[1]. Both these social groups desire a family that consists of only one son. Why has the preference for children been reduced to such a minimum in these communities?

To answer this question, one has to return to the question of how families consciously and unconsciously decide on the size and composition of their families. Indeed, this is the pressing question facing us as we try and understand why large parts of the country evince a strong preference for sons and have rapidly taken to new technologies which allow couples to control family size and achieve a desired family composition of mostly boys with one or no girl.

This article, instead of going into the details of the already existing rich research on the causes of son-preference, female infanticide and female foeticide, argues that, by concentrating entirely on the dyad of son-daughter, in which sons are preferred while daughters are not, we are missing out on significant gains yielded by taking other cross-generation and same generation members of the family into consideration. To develop our understanding, we need to take into account the varied roles men and women perform in the agrarian economy. Perhaps the key to the north Indian conundrum is not that sons are wanted and daughters are not, but that, daughters are not wanted while daughters-in-law are absolutely essential to the family. This will help explain the current "rush" to acquire brides from far-flung parts of the country by Haryanvis who have reduced their own female population to a pitiful 861 women for every 1,000 men. The article also argues that we are helped in solving the puzzle of long-standing female adverse sex ratios in the north and northwest by including in our analysis, family strategies *vis-á-vis,* the sons in the family. Historical and contemporary data shows that, the preference for sons is not as all-encompassing and undiluted as we have been led to think. Evidence is that, among large agrarian castes more than a certain number of sons was often frowned upon and the family's treatment of sons was often severely differentiated, privileging one or two sons, while others were left to

1 Stephanie Vella (2005) discusses the case of the gounders of Tamil Nadu. The information on Jat households is from fieldwork in Fatehgarh Sahib conducted as part of an Action Aid-funded project on adverse sex ratio (2007).

a lesser fate. There is no doubt, however that, unwanted sons did not meet the fate of an early death, which unwanted daughters did. Even today, a male foetus is rarely eliminated wilfully while innumerable female foetuses have been condemned to never being born as is made transparent in the recent censuses.

The article argues that for peasants in the northern countryside, especially those for whom fragmentation was a constant fear, the solution to the optimum family was not simply female infanticide but a combination of female infanticide and non-marriage of some sons. Both these strategies helped to reduce claimants on family resources. For men who were deliberately left unmarried, communities sanctioned fraternal polyandry in which the wife of the married brother was shared by the others. A certain number of men remained bachelors or entered into sexual liaisons with lower caste women but were not accorded a marriage of their own.

1. Existing Explanations for Daughter Elimination

Earlier research has suggested various reasons why families wanted fewer daughters than sons—(1) hypergamy—the need/desire to marry daughters into higher status families placed a burden on parents; (2) dowry—similarly needed to acquire desired grooms or to conform to "honourable" norms of marriage; these two "cultural" culprits have to be understood in relation to marriages as alliance building and ultimately as part of political strategies which may be accompanied by significant economic gains at the local and regional level; (3) women's lower value in wheat farming systems which require less of their labour or where their labour is less visible than in paddy farming systems; (4) seclusion or lack of participation in productive activities as an extension of the above (prevalent among certain northern high castes); (5) kinship, marriage and descent systems in which men inherit property and women move to unrelated and distant families to live with husbands; (6) patrilocality—the daughter moves to the husband's home and does not inherit immovable family property, and hence, is unable to either contribute to her natal family or offer old-age support to her parents which her brothers can; (7) furthermore, scholars such as Oldenburg (2002) provide a historical reason pointing out that the concentration of proprietary rights in the hands of individual males during the colonial period diluted unstated but, customarily recognised female rights in property contributing to their unwantedness. Other reasons, ritual and practical for needing more sons (including physical defence of the family and its assets) then become icing on the male privilege cake leading to daughters being considered the unwanted or burdensome children.

The historical record of female infanticide and excess female mortality in the north and north-west of India has been well-documented in the censuses conducted by the British and in independent India. Many scholars have analysed the female deficit (Agnihotri 2000; Bardhan 1974; Miller 1981; Mitra 2001; Vishwanath 2000, 2004, etc.) and noted regional and castewise patterns. In addition, several ethnographic works have documented and analysed the persistence of low sex ratios among dominant peasant castes or among some urban propertied groups. It is among the same groups today that infanticide has been largely replaced by elimination of female foetuses through sex-selective abortions, even as son-preference and declining sex ratios spread to other social groups earlier unaffected by it. Jeffery and Jeffery (1997) report a history of infanticide and low sex ratios for the jats of Bijnor in Uttar Pradesh. Pettigrew (1978) and Hershman (1981) note female infanticide and adelphic polyandry among the small landholder jats in Punjab.

Vishwanath (2004) discusses female infanticide in north and north-west, where not only elite rajputs, but also populous landowning groups like the lewa patidars, thakurs, jats, ahirs, khatris and gujjars practised female infanticide and had low sex ratios. More recent research confirms low sex ratios among the same groups—a survey in 10 villages in Morena in Madhya Pradesh showed child sex ratios of 392 among the gujjars, 400 among the yadavs, 417 among the rathors, 583 among the jats and 714 among the brahmins (Premi and Raju 1998). Linking female infanticide in the past with the present desire for an only son, family among the southern peasant group of the kongu vellalar gounders, Stephanie Vella says, "Moreover the ideal progeny in this community appears to be today that of a single child, preferably a male, and traditionally they had only two sons so as to avoid the division of land. Therefore, infanticide and abortion were perhaps above all a method of family planning in the absence of more modern means of contraception" (Vella: 2005) (or sex determination, one might add).

My concern is to explain the occurrence and persistence of daughter deficit among large peasant groups who are also generally the dominant castes in the northern part of the country. Some historians and demographers have contested sociological explanations which centre on hypergamy and dowry as the cause of female infanticide and neglect of daughters. They argue that this explanation—the pride (hypergamy) and purse (dowry)—as Miller (ibid) puts it, may fit upper castes such as rajputs who practised hypergamy and extreme female seclusion and hence, exclusion from "productive" work but does not explain rampant infanticide, neglect and contemporarily female foeticide among peasants with smaller holdings and little practice of hypergamy. In this context, Oldenburg (2002) argues that female infanticide was practised by isogamously marrying peasant castes for "family balancing" reasons and that dowry became a significant cause of female infanticide only with economic changes brought about by British colonial policies leading to a further tightening of the noose around the girl child. She rejects explanations forwarded by the British for female infanticide—hypergamy linked to dowry and expensive marriage celebrations. Caldwell *et. al.,* (1983) and Bhat and Halli (1999) also rebut the argument that dowry led to a desire for fewer daughters arguing instead that it was the shortage of marriageable men in the early part of the 20th century that led to the rise of dowry or groom price. Bhatt and Halli, however, attribute low sex ratios in the north/north-west to hypergamy and agree with most anthropologists that it led to infanticide of women at the top of the hierarchy (as it was difficult to find higher status grooms for women in the highest clans and keeping them unmarried was considered dishonourable) and breakdown of caste endogamy at the bottom (as women moved up, a shortage was created at the bottom rungs). Men of lower status or from poorer households had to pay brideprice or buy wives and make socially less desirable marriages.

Parry (1979) also reiterates the hypergamous marriage hypothesis for infanticide and neglect of girl children among the rathi rajputs of Kangra but, is unable to explain why the brahmins who also practised hypergamy did not kill their daughters, merely stating that the top group obviated this need by marrying them to equals. It is possible that the political gains yielded by hypergamous marriages were not of importance to brahmins who were rarely politically significant in the north and north-west. But, for most agrarian castes, especially dominant ones, hypergamous marriages were important for furthering status ambitions and were aspired to, by many; a point Oldenburg entirely misses in her desire to lay all blame at the door of the British. As Parry's discussion (ibid) of biradari reform and similar efforts in Gujarat discussed by Shah (1982) and documented for Punjab during the colonial period show, attempts at restricting hypergamy by making isogamous marriage mandatory within endogamous units and reducing marriage expenditure generally failed due to ambitions of deviating families. The same process is still visible among Haryanvi jat clans today.

2. Producing the 'Needed Family'

Many scholars seem to converge on the reasoning that the elimination of daughters had more to do with producing the kind of family agriculturists needed in the politico-economic terrain of the north and north-west. Such a family was definitely one with more boys and few girls. Miller (1981) calls it an indigenous form of family planning. DasGupta in her comparison of fertility decline in Punjab and Europe in the middle ages, states that household strategies to maintain a balance between population and resources in the first half of the 20th century, in the face of fluctuating numbers, included male celibacy (bachelorhood), reduction of female children through infanticide and neglect (since female non-marriage was not acceptable), informal polyandry or buying of wives when needed. According to her, marriage was also used as a strategy to control population. She argues that in recent times the successful control of women's fertility has made it possible to begin to reduce levels of permanent bachelorhood of men in this society (1995:491). Jeffery and Jeffery (ibid) made a similar argument for the jats of Bijnor in Uttar Pradesh and argued that, infanticide, neglect of girl children and non-marriage of men were strategies "to regulate population growth in the interests of conserving the resources of the lineage" (p 239). There evidence is trenchant because, it reflects a situation that has not changed from when it was first documented by the British in 1872. In 1990, they found that the demographic picture in the village they studied, Nangal, was still characterised by excess deaths of girl children and a relatively large number of unmarried adult jat men (ibid: 232). Jats and rajputs in villages of Etah district of Uttar Pradesh show similar patterns.

The ethnographies of peasant landowners in what was the undivided Punjab (Punjab, Himachal Pradesh and Haryana) appear to support the hypothesis that, infanticide, non-marriage of men and polyandry were strategies to control family numbers and that more importantly, these occurred together. Female infanticide or neglect of girl children were the tools adopted to keep the number of girls and women down. Equally, non-marriage of some sons was also a technique to limit the numbers of heirs and prevent fragmentation of land during the lifetime of brothers. Marriage of only one son also prevented infighting between brothers/couples which could lead to untimely subdivision of the land[2]. The key ethnographies available to us—Hershman (ibid) and Pettigrew (ibid) for Punjabi Jats, testify to the extensive practice of surreptitious polyandry among them. Thus, Hershman says "Polyandry is a recognised state of affairs in Punjabi society and it is basically condoned" (p 187). Pettigrew, who conducted fieldwork not just in one village but in a large area states that, she came across numerous instances of a woman being married to one brother (p 53). Even though society disapproved of the practice, it accepted its widespread occurrence among agricultural castes. The patterns among the jats were often emulated in the caste of agricultural labourers, the chamars, across the north Indian plains.

3. The Dispensability of Daughters

While providing a plausible explanation, these arguments do not succeed in laying out why it was daughters who needed to be got rid of if it, was a matter of keeping a balance between resources and humans. Yet, it is clear that between sons and daughters, daughters were more dispensable and more burdensome and less valued and hence, the ones to be culled while men were simply left unmarried. It has been mentioned that while men could be left unmarried so that they reproduced only through a single wife held in common, the marriage of all daughters was a must. Among some high status families within clans it was also important that women be married into families of higher standing than their own. The necessity of marriage of daughters and in the case of higher status women, of an appropriate marriage, provide some of the reasons for why it was thought better to get rid of

2 North India largely followed the Mitakshara system of inheritance in which all sons became heirs to ancestral property at birth. Hence, the peasant was always fearful of land fragmenting into economically unviable holdings if the number of sons was too large. Keeping some sons unmarried, as elaborated later, also served the purpose of reducing the number of heirs. According to informants, the new inheritance laws which favour the equal division of property between sons and daughters are causing further upheaval in the north-Indian countryside. The share of land inherited by daughters is being reverted back to sons/brothers with payment of prohibitive transfer costs. This is possibly another reason for the tightening of the noose around the female foetus (Field notes from Action Aid Project in Fatehgarh Sahib, Punjab).

daughters at birth. But, it still does not answer the question as to why middle peasants who were not beholden to marrying their daughters into higher status families or who could even receive a bride price for their daughters would kill them. In such families, the labour of women was also a necessity unlike among the elite rajputs where the extreme seclusion of women rendered them economically "useless". While bringing the so-called "cultural" explanation of hypergamy and the necessity of marriage of women back into the picture, it is important to take a clue from Parry (ibid) and a recent paper by Chakraborty and Kim (2008) which points to the close links between kinship and marriage and the stability of northern political systems. Hypergamy was a major political strategy of clans and political power more often than not also brought economic gains with it.

4. Daughters vs Daughters-in-law

In the following sections, let me put forward my hypothesis which I feel, adds something to the existing explanations of daughter elimination. I am suggesting that to gain an explanation of daughter dispreference, we need to look at a broader matrix of roles and relationships than simply the sons vs daughters axis. We need to look at the whole gamut of relationships in the family—the husband-wife dyad, the father-son dyad (or by extension brother-brother) and interestingly, the mother-in-law-daughter-in-law dyad. This is obviously a simplified model/ sketch since families will consist of multiple sons, daughters-in-law, etc. The point being made is that, to produce a peasant family necessary to run the peasant farm, the basic unit necessary is not merely the agnatic unit of landholders, but that it is important to consider individuals in their various roles. Men are equally important in the role of fathers/husbands/sons and we have to recognise that women are crucial to this perpetuation in their role as wives/daughters-in-law. Obviously, the glaringly missing figure here is that of the daughter/sister. Why is she missing, is she not in anyway necessary to the family?

First, let us see why the others are necessary in the landscape of north/north-west India. The labour of males is necessary although there might be differentiation as discussed below as to the value of the labour of different brothers. The male as husband, father and son is necessary in a patriarchal, patrilineal system to run the farm, to keep it viable and to inherit land and reproduce the family, to pass on the land to. Additionally, it is important to recognise that peasant agriculture is dependent on both female and male labour. That female labour in the north may not be given the recognition it deserves is another matter (cf Miller 1981). But, in the landscape of the small peasant family farm, both men and women are equally needed to make the land viable. The woman is responsible for several supporting activities and even main activities without which the family farm would collapse. Indeed, this is what makes marriage an "economic necessity" and leads to recognition of the worth of the wife if not of the daughter. Especially, in agricultural systems, in which crop growing and animal husbandry are combined and symbiotically linked, an enormous amount of labour falls upon the woman's shoulders. Folk wisdom recognises it and so did Malcolm Darling when he said that, the farmer would soon lose his land if he did not have a wife. He attributes a man's inability to pay his revenue dues to his single status, since an "akela aadmi" (bachelor) would not be able to perform well agriculturally; and a widower was considered to be "half-paralysed" (Darling 1925, 1977: p 53). Indeed, the British encouraged widowers and widows to remarry. Leviratic marriage of the widow ensured that her labour would remain in the family and her claims to manage land on behalf of a young son and thus gain control over it, would be blunted. Buying of brides and bride-price practices which appeared appalling to the British initially were ultimately tolerated since they kept revenues flowing (Chowdhry 2007).

Among women's roles, the role of the wife is equally important as a producer and a reproducer. She is the biological reproducer of sons and hence of the family, even if the family is "socially" reproduced by the man. When a woman grows old, these roles are taken over in the family, not by her daughter but by the daughter-in-law, the son's wife (Chowdhry on the importance of the daughter-in-law: 1994:50). Hence, wives have always been needed even if not too many. The number of wives brought in could easily be controlled by the family, but the birth of excess daughters could only be controlled through infanticide or neglect. The number of wives and reproducers could be kept down by allowing brothers to share one wife[3]. But if the family needed another wife and one was not easily available in the community (due to daughters being killed or married into higher status groups) or was too expensive, she could be recruited from another caste or

[3] Berreman's work on Himalyan polyandry (1975) clearly outlines the context in which the system flourishes. Wives are recruited to the group as and when needed and polyandry serves a useful purpose if men have to practise multiple livelihood strategies of which male migration is one.

even from a long distance. A wife's duties were made clear to her and the wife who did not produce children, especially sons was in danger of being sent back or supplemented with a co-wife. A woman who was widowed and did not have male heirs would either be married to the brother of the deceased man or sent back to her natal home (Hershman 1981, Chowdhry 1994).

Thus, if one goes over the "needed" members and the "needed" roles, the one that is conspicuously missing from the scene is the daughter/sister. It is eminently clear that while a son can take over the father's mantle—his position and his role in the natal family (and this is ritualised in north India in the "pagri-rasam" through which the transfer is effected after the death of the father, making the son the *de facto* head of the family (rather than the surviving mother), the daughter cannot take over the mother's. The son can reproduce the father's family but the daughter cannot reproduce her parental family. Her reproductive labour belongs to another family, i.e., consanguine women cannot reproduce the lineage. Her productive labour may be of some use to her family—in some communities she is allowed to contribute her labour until she marries or during frequent visits to the natal home in the early years of marriage (Palriwala 2001). But often these visits are interpreted by the daughter as well-deserved periods of rest from the hard labour endured in the marital home. In the past, marriage at an early age ensured that she did not provide help for long although there are instances in which the marriage of a daughter is delayed either because parents need her labour or need time to accumulate an adequate dowry. In her in-laws family, the new bride immediately takes on, first the domestic tasks, then farm tasks, and the sooner she proves her fecundity by bearing a child, preferably a son, the better it is for her.

So, it is the daughter-in-law who steps into the mother's shoes as she takes on the productive and reproductive roles of her mother-in-law. Thus, wives and daughters-in-law, though they may be disliked and often barely tolerated and though their status may remain uncertain until they become mothers and mothers-in-law themselves, are needed and acquired somehow or the other. A reading of the history of jats and other agricultural groups shows that, not all families among them could afford to be punctilious about where they got their wives from or how. Hence, the easy violation of caste and other social injunctions among these groups as far as marriage was concerned. Jats and rajputs in Punjab were known to marry into castes below them and even intermarry with women from the untouchable castes (Hershman: ibid 180, Parry ibid, Chowdhry 2007). In fact, most ethnographic evidence points to the tolerance of a variety of marriage forms—with or without dowry, bride-price marriages, hypergamous and isogamous marriages, those conforming to the norms of endogamy and those violating them, existing in the same space. What kind of a marriage a family or a man made depended on his socio-economic circumstances and comparable status goals.

The desperate need for brides and daughters-in-law is underlined in contemporary Haryana and Punjab states, suffering from acute bride-shortage due to their extremely skewed sex ratios. In these states, men are bringing as wives women from states as far-flung as Assam, West Bengal, Kerala and Maharashtra, women with whom they share neither language nor culture. Even their caste and religion does not matter (Kaur 2004, 2007). In Morena, a low sex ratio district in Madhya Pradesh, when families were asked who they would marry their sons to, if there were no girls, the answer was that, girls would come from "other families" (Field notes from Action Aid Project 2007).

To put it crudely and instrumentally, while families may love their daughters, daughters are the only "dispensable" members of the family. Not only are they structurally dispensable (looked at from the point of view of a single family or household) but they represent "outgoings" as far as household resources are concerned in contrast to sons[4]. And, if one is balancing members against resources, then fewer daughters are better and if there are none, then there is generally no regret. People go to extreme lengths to procure a son—in the old days, through frequent and prolonged childbearing, in contemporary times, by undergoing repeated abortions of female foetuses—but there is no pressing desire to have a girl. More recently, even older couples in Punjab who are well past their child-bearing years are trying to have sons with the help of expensive assisted

[4] Daughters are popularly referred to as 'paraya dhan' or as guests in their own natal homes. In China, another country with a low sex ratio, bringing up a daughter is referred to as "watering the neighbour's garden". Even though the society needs daughters who will become daughters-in-law, each family sees itself as not needing daughters and needing only daughters-in-law. In Gujarat (Mehsana district), another state suffering from low sex ratios, exchange marriage (known as 'ata-sata', in Punjab as 'vatasata') in which a family gives a daughter in exchange for a daughter-in-law is becoming common. Families with no daughters have to pay bride-price or marry women from lower castes or tribal communities or their sons have to remain bachelors.

reproductive technologies. As one such man, Makhan Singh of Gurdaspur district, said "Only a son can wipe the paap (sin) of childlessness" Makhan Singh is 57 and his wife is 51 and they were visiting a fertility clinic to try and have a child (son) (*India Today*, December 22, 2003). The felt ritual value of a daughter earning merit through kanyadaan is fast disappearing. The son's importance is continually reiterated including in his role as a brother. Most north Indian families express the view that a brother is necessary to facilitate the marriages of sisters.

5. Are All Sons Wanted?

The demonstrated unwantedness of girls should not blind us to the fact that historically and contemporarily, there has not been unadulterated love for more than the necessary number of sons among farming communities. Proverbs from Punjab and Haryana warn against too many sons, even as the ideal family continues to be the one consisting of more sons than daughters[5]. In Bhagwatipur village, in Rohtak district of Haryana, a pandit family was not thrilled when the wife gave birth to twin boys at her third pregnancy recently. One of the sons was subsequently sent to her parent's home (AA Project Rohtak 2007). While sons may not ever be eliminated at birth or their birth actively prevented, not all were/are granted equal status in the family. These less-favoured sons are often second class citizens within the household. The family deliberately chooses to let them remain bachelors or tries to disinherit them or makes them share one wife. Basically, they are reduced to what the Chinese call "bare branches"—men who will not have families of their own. In the Indian countryside they are referred to as "bechara" (one without food or resources). "Bachelors are much pitied in Pandit society" wrote Madan in his study of Kashmiri pandits (1965:101). Most ethnographies of the Punjab region document the phenomenon of the bachelor brother who was a marginal member of the household; his well-being dependent on how much land he stood to inherit and who among the other brothers coveted his share of the land and thus consented to take care of him. In Haryana, I was told by an informant that the status of a bachelor is that of a family servant.

[5] Prem Chowdhry (1994:50) quotes a proverb from Haryana which translates as "A daughter after two sons brings prosperity. Three sons in a row bring beggary." Interestingly, Miller reports a study by Smith for 18th century Japan which showed that the Nakaharans practised a sort of family planning which was integrally related to the needs of agricultural production such that children not needed were killed. The author found evidence of male infanticide, generally of later-born males even though female infanticide was preponderant [Miller: 1981: 43]. She also quotes a study by Beals in south India where medical care given to girls and to later-born boys showed that both were less desired (ibid:101).

According to another informant, bachelors are often not allowed into the house—they are sent food in the 'gher' (cattle shed). In Punjab, they similarly spent their lives in the cattle shed, called the haveli. A jat Sikh woman respondent while describing her husband's father's brother who remained unmarried said "he was not given any share in the land. So far as his living was concerned, he used to shift from one place to the other; sometimes at the Gurdwara, at times he would live with his sister or with his brother" (AA Project, Fatehgarh Sahib 2007). In the Haryana field site, murders and suicides of bachelors were reported (village Bhagwatipur, Rohtak district, AA Project 2007).

The incidence of bachelorhood (referred to as celibacy by some demographers) in north India—7 per cent in the age group 45-54 in 1911 (Bhat and Halli 1999) in contrast to 3 per cent in the south pointed to a substantial number of unmarried men. The presence of unmarried men has been documented by a large number of ethnographic studies in the north (Darling 1925, Parry ibid, Jeffery and Jeffery: ibid, Minturn 1993 and others) with the result that a stratification of men emerged within families and endogamous groups—those who got to marry and those who did not[6]. The kind of marriage various men merited could also vary. Pierre Bourdieu, commenting on the differential fates of older and younger brothers in Algerian peasant families says "More over, although there is no official recognition of any privilege for the eldest (of the boys, of course), everything conspires to favour him to the detriment of his younger brothers, to marry him first and as well as possible, that is, outside rather than inside the lineage, the younger brothers being destined for production rather than the exchanges of the marriage market or assembly, for work on land rather than the house's external politics" (1977:69).[7]

---

6 In the south, among the famous case of nambudiri brahmins, only the eldest son was allowed to marry a nambudiri woman. The other brothers had liaisons with nayar women [Gough: 1959]. A M Shah mentions a caste in Gujarat in which the eldest son remains, by custom, a bachelor, but succeeds the father as the head of the joint family with legal and moral authority. At death his corpse is first ritually married to a sacred plant in the crematorium and then cremated (personal communication, March 23, 2008). Praveena Kodoth (2006) mentions the opposite for nambudiri women who were not married even though the eldest marrying male could practise polygyny. For women who were left spinsters, a marriage ceremony had to be performed when they died and before they were cremated. These cultural requirements point to the importance of marriage as a lifecycle phase and to the reality of family marriage strategies which left certain men or women married.

7 Recent research in Rohtak district of Haryana reveals that after the marriage of the first son, the marriages of subsequent sons may be simple affairs. The method followed is that of "chunni charana"—a group of five individuals goes to the bride's house, a simple ceremony consisting of an exchange of garlands takes place and the bride is brought home. A full ceremonial marriage is not performed because, "social obligations" have been taken care of by the first son's marriage.

Demographers and sociologists have remarked how the shortage of women impinges negatively on men who are on the bottom rungs—whether of the family or of the clan. Men who are less desirable—who lack land, education, are jobless or have been tinged by scandal, are the ones who cannot find brides. My recent studies of long-distance marriage in Haryana and Uttar Pradesh (2004, 2007) reveal that it is sons who are unable to get local wives due to the acute shortage of women and whose families make little attempt to find them spouses, who arrange their own marriages with women from Assam, West Bengal, Maharashtra and Kerala. In doing so, they are apparently circumventing the family's strategies to balance resources and family size. With individuals being less governed by the family, this shows the active agency of men in not leaving their fate in the hands of the family—parents or married brothers. An equally important factor is the contemporary marginalization of the bachelor in the rural household. As Amar Kaur, an elderly woman of the balmiki caste in Sirhind district of Punjab remarked, no doubt, in the past too there were bachelors but not as many as today. But, what is important to note is that, "previously, neither there used to be any fight over the distribution of land nor the women used to hesitate in giving food to the unmarried men. Instead, the unmarried men had a status in the house; even after they were dead they were respected. The women of today will swear a hundred times before giving food to their younger brother-in-law" (Action Aid Adverse Sex Ratio Project 2007).

Amar Kaur's views point to the transformation occurring in rural areas where effective nuclearization of family relationships is taking place even within the joint family structure. It is the conjugal relationship that is gaining in importance in contrast to the earlier emphasis on the agnatic bond. As couples focus more on the well-being and aspirations of their biological children and on the nuclear unit they tend to ignore obligatory relationships with unmarried siblings and even old parents. The demographically small-sized modern family has less time, space and resources for those outside its immediate circle.

While marriage of all sons upsets familial calculations of sustenance from the land, it explains the acute urgency and need for men to find off-farm sources of livelihood. The desire for government jobs, the investing of large sums of money to purchase public sector jobs such as those of havaldars or in the army, points to the necessity for small holders to diversify livelihood strategies. It is interesting that the discourse of non-marriage of males and the difficulties of finding brides in Haryana today is tied not to its abysmal sex ratios but to unemployment. It is often claimed in Haryana today that as soon as a man finds a job he will get several offers of marriage. In the family, male livelihood insecurities indirectly feed into a sharpening of son-preference and instigate higher investments in male children as the family continues to repose hope for support in the male.

Even among seemingly well-to-do agriculturists such as jats in the north and gounders in the south, it is the real and perceived precariousness of agricultural livelihoods that explains the desire for a family consisting of a single son. As the benchmark for living standards continues to rise and with it the cost of living and agricultural yields plateau, the desire is to put all eggs in the basket of a single son. As older generations informed me in Fatehgarh district of Punjab, the younger child-bearing generations have no fear of the mortality of this one son. Parents of single sons amplified on the costs of education and the unviability of holdings if more than one son was produced. Data from our study in Fatehgarh Sahib district of Punjab (the district with the lowest sex ratio in the country in the 2001 Census) reveals that if the first child is a son, the parents believe that the family is complete. In such a scenario the question of wanting a daughter does not even arise. This is the phenomenon of the "selfinflicted" one-son family. With the desire for zero daughters, the task of redressing the sex ratio imbalance becomes even more daunting and consequently our strategies for preventing daughter elimination need to be much more radical than those presently in operation.

(Ravinder Kaur is with the Department of Humanities and Social Sciences, Indian Institute of Technology, New Delhi. She can be reached at ravinder.iitd@gmail.com).

References

Action Aid/IDRC (2007): 'Addressing Adverse Sex Ratio in Selected Districts of Himachal Pradesh, Madhya Pradesh, Rajasthan, Punjab and Haryana', Unpublished Country Reports from the Study.

Agnihotri, Satish (2000): *Sex Ratio Patterns in the Indian Population: A Fresh Exploration*, Sage Publications, New Delhi.

Bardhan, P K (1974): 'On Life and Death Questions' in *Economic & Political Weekly*, Special Issue No. 9:1293-1304.

Bhat, Mari P N and S S Halli (1999): 'Demography of Brideprice and Dowry: Causes and Consequences of the Indian Marriage Squeeze' in *Population Studies*, Vol. 53, No 2, July, pp 129-48.

Berreman, G D (1975): 'Himalayan Polyandry and the Domestic Cycle' in P Uberoi (ed) (1993), *Family, Kinship and Marriage in India*, Oxford University Press, Delhi.

Bourdieu, Pierre (1977): *Outline of a Theory of Practice*, Cambridge University Press, Cambridge.

Caldwell, J C, P H Reddy and P Caldwell (1983): 'The Causes of Marriage Change in South India', *Population Studies* 37 (4), pp 343-61.

Chakraborty, Tanika and Sukkoo Kim (2008): 'Caste, Kinship and Sex Ratios in India', Working Paper 13828, National Bureau of Economic Research, *http://www.nber.org/papers/w13828.*

Chowdhry, Prem (1994): *The Veiled Women*, Oxford University Press, New Delhi.

– (2007): 'Fluctuating Fortunes of Wives: Creeping Rigidity in Inter-caste Marriages in the Colonial Period' in *The Indian Historical Review*, Vol. XXX, No. 1, January, pp 210-43.

Darling, Malcolm Lyall (1925): *The Punjab Peasant in Prosperity and Debt*, Manohar (1977 edition), Delhi.

DasGupta, M (1995): 'Fertility Decline in Punjab, India: Parallels with Historical Europe' in *Population Studies*, 49, pp 481-500.

Gough, Kathleen (1959): 'The Nayars and the Definition of Marriage' in P Uberoi (ed), *Family, Kinship and Marriage in India*, 1993, Oxford University Press, Delhi.

Hershman, Paul (1981): *Punjabi Kinship and Marriage*, Hindustan Publishing Corporation, Delhi.

Jeffery, Roger and Patricia Jeffery (1997): *Population, Gender and Politics*, Cambridge University Press, Cambridge.

Kaur, Ravinder (2004): 'Across Region Marriages – Poverty, Female Migration and the Sex Ratio' in *Economic & Political Weekly*, Vol. XXXIX, No. 25, pp 2595-603.

– (2007): 'Declining Juvenile Sex Ratios: Economy, Society and Technology, Explanations from Field Evidence' in *Margin – The Journal of Applied Economic Research*, 1:2, pp 231-45, Sage Publications, Los Angeles/London/New Delhi/Singapore.

– (2007): 'The Shortage of Spouses, Marriage Strategies and the Sex Ratio: An Examination of Cross-Region Marriages in Haryana', unpublished paper presented at Jawaharlal Nehru University on September 3.

Kodoth, Praveena (2006): 'Producing a Rationale for Dowry? Gender in the Negotiation of Exchange at Marriage in Kerala, South India', *www. lse.ac.uk/collections/asia* Research Centre.

Miller, Barbara D (1981): *The Endangered Sex: Neglect of Female Children in Rural North India*, Cornell University Press, Ithaca.

Mitra, Ashok (2001): 'Implications of Declining Sex Ratio in India' in Vina Mazumdar and N Krishnaji (eds), *Enduring Conundrum: India's Sex Ratio*, Rainbow Publishers, Delhi.

Minturn, Leigh (1993): *Sita's Daughters: Coming out of Purdah*, Oxford University Press, New York.

Oldenburg, Veena (2002): *Dowry Murder: The Imperial Origins of a Cultural Crime*, Oxford University Press, New Delhi.

Palriwala, R (2001): 'Transitory Residents, Invisible Workers: Rethinking Locality and Incorporation in a Rajasthan Village' in K Sangari and U Chakravarti (eds), *From Myths to Markets*, Manohar Publishers, New Delhi.

Parry, Jonathan (1979): *Caste and Kinship in Kangra*, Routledge and Kegan Paul, London.

Premi, M K and Saraswati Raju (1998): 'Born to Die: Female Infanticide in Madhya Pradesh' in *Search Bulletin*, July-September 13, (3).

Pettigrew, Joyce (1978): *Robber Noblemen: A Study of the Political System of the Sikh Jats*, Ambika Publishers, New Delhi.

Shah, A M (1982): 'Division and Hierarchy: An Overview of Caste in Gujarat' in *Contributions to Indian Sociology* (NS), Vol. 16, No. 1.

Vella, Stephanie (2005): 'Low Fertility and Female Discrimination in South India: The Puzzle of Salem District, Tamil Nadu' in C Z Guilmoto and S Irudaya Rajan (eds), *Fertility Transition in South India*, Sage Publications, New Delhi.

Vinayak, Ramesh (2003): 'Grand Old Parents' in *India Today*, December 22.

Vishwanath, L S (2000): *Female Infanticide and Social Structure*, Hindustan Publishing Corporation, Delhi.

– (2004): 'Female Infanticide: The Colonial Experience' in *Economic & Political Weekly*, May 29.

10

Missing Women and Brides from Faraway
Social Consequences of the Skewed Sex Ratio in India

Ravinder Kaur

The growing flexibility in gender roles is yet to be reflected in change in societal perceptions which continue to consider men as the ideal breadwinner and women as eventual contributors only to their in-laws families. China reported shortage of brides leading to cross border marriages, abduction of women and return to traditional system, where families would adopt infant girls to raise them as future brides for their sons. The social structure and culture intertwined to make sons highly valued while daughters were correspondingly devalued. Families feel a pressing need to invest in the success of sons especially in the absence of social security systems for parents. The article highlights the sex determination technologies which allowed people to retain male and abort female foetuses.

Source: www.hw.oeaw.ac.at, AAS Working Papers in Social Anthropology edited by Andre Gingrich & Helmut Lukas.

Missing Women in India and China

The economist Amartya Sen brought international attention to the problem of 'missing women' by calculating that there were 100 million women less in the world (Sen: 1990). These missing women turned out to be primarily from large Asian countries such as India and China and some smaller countries such as South Korea and Taiwan. The world was shocked by this unnatural deficit and scholars began to initiate research into how we could have arrived at this state of affairs. At around the same time, media began to focus on the spread of sex-determination technologies which allowed people to retain male and abort female foetuses. Reports also began to trickle in of the excess of bachelors in several of these countries. In China, the bride shortage was reported to have led to cross-border marriages, abduction of women and even a return to a traditional system in which families would adopt infant girls to raise them as future brides for their sons (DasGupta and Li Shuzhuo: 1999). In India, there were evidences of a return to fraternal polyandry and import of wives from other cultural regions within the country (Kaur: 2004).

In the first part of the article, I discuss reasons for adverse sex ratios in these countries and in the second part its implications for marriage. While the article deals primarily with India, a few comments are made regarding China in the first section. Social scientists, demographers and gender specialists began to worry about this deficit in the female population for several reasons. First, adverse sex ratios are a manifest indicator of an increase rather than a decline in gender inequality. Second, even more worrisome, why and how was it that women and girls were disappearing in the population as these countries progressed economically? India, China, South Korea and Taiwan, have all shown spectacular economic gains in recent decades. As more women got educated, joined the workforce, the expectation was that, traditional gender inequalities would lessen. With the rising age at marriage and lowered fertility, women would be able to participate in the public domain on an equal footing. There would be improvements in their hitherto lower status. The declining female sex ratios point to the contrary—to specific forms of discrimination which have emerged or got strengthened even as women make some progress in a number of domains.

According to demographers, China developed highly masculine sex ratios as a result of its aggressive one-child policy (the present sex ratio in China being 856 girls to a 1000 boys). India, the other large contributor showed a secular decline in its sex ratio over the past century with a slight improvement appearing in the latest census conducted in 2001 (from 927 in 1991 to 933 in 2001). Traditionally and even up to the present, despite differing religions, India and China have been large patriarchal peasant societies with a culture and tradition of 'son-preference'. The patrilineal social structure in both societies supported inheritance primarily for men; in return, men were responsible for supporting parents in old age. Women moved away at marriage from their natal to their conjugal homes (patrivirilocality), generally residing with in-laws. Parents were thus deprived of any further advantage from them. Men also had religious duties towards parents during death rites, considered especially important in India. The social structure and culture thus intertwined to make sons highly valued while daughters were correspondingly devalued. Although China practises bride-price as marriage payment and India dowry (an additional reason for viewing daughters as burdensome), sex ratios in both countries show a devaluation of women's contributions.

Modern Sex-Determination Technologies and Female Deficits

A recent paper in the *Lancet* (Jha *et. al.,* 2006) concluded that the decline in girl children in India could largely be attributed to sex selective abortions and that in the last two decades, ten million female foetuses had been aborted in India. In both China and India, the introduction of NRTs (New Reproductive Technologies) has aided the sharp decline in juvenile sex ratios. China introduced ultrasound testing of pregnancies as part of enforcing its one-child policy. In India, from the late 1970s onwards, various methods of sex determination gained ground. Beginning with amniocentesis and Chorion Villous Sampling (CVS), what slowly gained popularity was ultrasonography which allowed the detection of the sex of the child without an invasive procedure (Croll: 2000, Patel: 2007). Ultrasounds, although reliable only after the first trimester of the pregnancy, were cheap and easily available. In India especially, unscrupulous medical practitioners, radiologists and gynaecologists cashed into Indian couples' desire to have sons by providing ultrasound testing even in remote villages by making testing facilities available in small towns and through mobile ultrasound units.

Modern sex-determination technology has largely supplanted traditional means of daughter elimination such as female infanticide. India has been known to have several regions where female infanticide was practiced (Punjab, Haryana, Rajasthan, Madhya Pradesh, Gujarat and certain pockets of Tamil Nadu such as Salem and Dharmapuri) historically. While the practice is minimal now, deliberate neglect of girl children continues to add to their attrition. Deprivation of nutrition and health care leads to higher rates of girl child mortality while maternal mortality as a cause of death still remains high in several adverse sex ratio areas.

'Family Planning' and 'Planning the Family'

The new technology of ultrasound has made it easier for couples to plan families with the sex composition of their choice. In India, the two child norm encouraged by the Government of India as its official policy for 'population stabilization' has led to a substantial decline in fertility across the country. However, in the North West of India, this policy has worked against the girl child. As family size declined, North Indian couples chose to retain their preference for boys, eliminating girl children before birth through the use of ultrasound technology. In fact, during the early period of introduction of sex determination technologies, doctors recommended this as a means of reducing India's burgeoning population. So little were they aware of the ethical dimensions and of a future in which ruthless elimination of female foetuses would become the common scenario. Recent feminist critiques of national family planning policies have argued that these were designed and implemented without any thought towards gender equality or taking into consideration existing societal structures which privileged men over women, boys over girls.

The use of technological methods of sex-determination and daughter elimination has allowed society to deploy the rhetoric of 'choice' in planning family size and composition. Accordingly, it is 'modern' to have small families and even better to be able to choose the sex of the offspring. In this way, families would not have to subject themselves to excessive unwanted fertility in the search for sons or subject themselves to the guilt of infanticide. Statistical data shows that the higher the educational level of the mother, more prone she is to using sex-determination and eliminating unwanted girl children in order to have the size and sex composition that the family wishes to achieve (DasGupta: 1987, Guilmoto: 2007).

Development, Prosperity and Adverse Sex Ratios

Demographers and sociologists (Agnihotri: 2000, Bose: 2001, Kaur: 2007) have pointed to the negative correlation between higher levels of development, prosperity and balanced sex ratios. Thus in India, the prosperous states of Punjab, Haryana, Maharashtra and Gujarat and rich cities like Chandigarh and Delhi show the worst sex ratios. These areas have high per capita incomes, fairly high levels of literacy and greater access to health facilities. It is thus a conundrum as to why conventional economic development is not translating into human or social development and why in such areas there is harsher discrimination against girl children. This is revealed in the shocking decline in child sex ratios—the ratio dropped by 82 points in Punjab and by 59 points in Haryana (Bose: 2001). Prosperity should ideally translate into non-discrimination especially when there are fewer children. However, this has palpably not turned out to be case in North India.

Scholars have attempted to explain the further decline of child sex ratios in prosperous areas in terms of access to education, information and technology in the context of the transition to a small family size. These factors may provide the mechanism of the decline but do not explain why girls are considered burdensome when people are rich and girls themselves are more literate and capable of financial independence. How and why then is son-preference getting reinforced? The explanation may lie in the intersection of political economy with the institutions of family and marriage. The narrowing of the gender gap between men and women is being achieved within social structural conditions which leave gender relations unequal and unchanged and existing political economic conditions often strengthen these. Property and inheritance relations while legally more gender-equal now continue to be practised within a patrilineal ideology. The growing flexibility in gender roles is yet to be reflected in change in societal perceptions which continue to construct men as the ideal bread-winner and women as eventual contributors only to their in-laws' families. Increasing land fragmentation and slow growth of employment opportunities for educated males make families perceive economic conditions as being especially insecure for males who continue to be perceived as the main bread-winners and status-carriers for the family. Hence, families feel a pressing need to invest in the success of sons, especially in the absence of social security systems for parents.

In keeping with the above, inter-generational entitlements of boys are considered to be an 'investment' while those of girls are considered to be 'expenditure' and a drain on family resources. The Indian daughter typically is considered to be a 'guest' in her own home until she is married and sent to her husband's home. Thus investment in her accrues to her husband's family as does the dowry essential for a culturally 'honourable' marriage. Also contributing to the perception of how entitlements in children of different sexes are viewed is evaluation of female and male worth in other spheres. Women's work, which is often unpaid, underpaid or homebased or paid in kind, is not given the same value as that of males. Hence, the perception of the male as the true breadwinner continues. This justifies higher household allocations of food, nutrition and health entitlements in the boy than in the girl. The net result of higher valuation of the boy is that, mothers who bear sons are glorified and attain a high status in society while those who bear only girls or are infertile are devalued. Women and girl children internalize this differential value and in turn devalue their own sex.

Social Consequences – Bride Shortage and Marriage Migration

As the number of girls in the society declines, several serious consequences are plainly in view. A foremost worry is that, development gains and progress made by women such that, they are no longer burdened with early marriage and high fertility and a narrowing of the gender gap in education etc., may be reversed in such a climate. The age at marriage for women may come down once again (we see evidence of a marginal decline in the state of Haryana, between 1991 and 2001). This will negatively impact their education and workforce participation. Girls and women may be forced back into exclusively domestic roles and there might be greater sexual demands on them. Shortage of girls, instead of making them more valued can intensify violence against them as they become a 'scarce' commodity.

A very visible effect facing several states is the excess of bachelors and problems in finding brides. In Indian society where social adulthood arrives only with marriage, the prospect of non-marriage becomes a serious matter. In rural areas, marriage is also necessary for making farming viable. Hence, the marriage squeeze against men (shortage of brides) is impacting society in various ways. In a society with both positive and negative rules of marriage (caste endogamy, clan and village exogamy, hypergamy, marriage accompanied by dowry, an appropriate age gap between spouses, arranged marriage etc.,) are rigidly enforced, the marriage market becomes 'tight', making it even more difficult for men to find spouses.

As a consequence of the adverse female sex ratio, men in the states of Haryana and Punjab are experiencing a nearly twenty percent deficit of marriageable women. Thus, given current sex ratios, one in every five men would remain unmarried. This situation will worsen considerably in the future with the recent declines in child sex ratios. In Haryana, men who reach the age of thirty five and are still single are unable to find a local bride. Men who become widowers cannot marry again. Under these circumstances, the society has developed a number of 'coping' mechanisms. These, as will be clearly realized in the discussion below are neither female nor family friendly.

In the North-West of India, parts of which have had more than a century of skewed sex ratios, men have long had to cope with female spousal shortages. Two solutions were common—involuntary bachelorhood or celibacy and fraternal polyandry. Given small landholdings and shortage of brides, families practised what Bourdieu (1977) calls the "collective strategies of the group involved" as a result of which many men were forced to remain single. They survived as adjuncts to their married brother/s families. Often, they were accommodated not in the main dwelling but in the dwelling meant for the cattle (*haveli* in Punjab and *gher* in Haryana). The married brother who accommodated the bachelor usually hoped to inherit his share of the land.

Surreptitious Polyandry

Polyandry or rather 'surreptitious' or informal polyandry was the other modality of accommodating bachelors in the family. Generally, the eldest brother would marry with the understanding that the wife would be shared by the other brothers. This system is not akin to what Berreman (1975) describes for the lower Himalayas where a number of factors perpetuated what he calls 'polygynyandry'. Pettigrew (1975) and Hershman (1981) have both discussed the prevalence of polyandry in Punjabi villages, especially among the Jat landowning agriculturists and the agricultural labourers, the Chamars. Both scholars point to the fact that while it existed due to a combination of shortage of girls and concerns over land fragmentation, it was not readily admitted to. Jeffery and Jeffery (1997) draw a similar scenario for the Jats of Western Uttar Pradesh who suffer from similar spousal shortages.

Census estimates for the past century rarely showed any unmarried women in the North of India while a certain percentage of men always remained unmarried (DasGupta: 1995, Bhatt and Halli:1999). Given the scarcity of women, widows in landowning communities, were strictly 'husbanded' by being married in leviratic relationships to a younger brother of the dead husband or even to a married older brother. This was in stark contrast to ideal Hindu custom which prohibited widow remarriage. Prem Chowdhry (1994), while documenting the diversity of marriage arrangements in Haryanvi society, has argued that during the colonial period marriages that violated superior (or upper caste) social norms were increasingly discredited and both caste and marriage norms came to be rigidly enforced. While the tradition of widow remarriage remained intact, polyandrous relationships declined. Intercaste marriage also declined during the colonial period and in the present day, Haryana couples in intercaste marriages are severely punished, often to the point of death (Chowdhry: 2007). More recently, there is information that given severely constrained circumstances of bride-shortage, families are again allowing the practice of polyandry.

'Import' of Cross-Region Brides

With few local brides at hand, men who are at risk of remaining unmarried are practising a third solution—marrying out of region or 'importing' brides from other regions. This is what I turn to now. Increasingly, men in Haryana are seeking brides from the Eastern and Southern region of India. Brides have thus been acquired from the Eastern states of Assam, West Bengal, Tripura, from the Southern states of Kerala and Andhra Pradesh and even from the Western state of Maharashtra. In Haryana, there have been some long standing patterns of brides coming from Assam and West Bengal. However, more recently in a desperate attempt, men are seeking brides wherever they can find them.

The marriage distance in such unions far exceeds that of the normal radius for alliances, in some cases requiring several days journey by train. In marrying so far from home, couples are crossing cultural regions with the result that they share nothing in common—they speak different languages, eat different food, wear different clothes and their behavioural-cultural norms are distinctive. Living together involves considerable adjustment for the couple and raises concerns over the acceptance of such marriages and especially over the status of children of such unions. Women especially face difficulties and the early years of marriage are very hard. Yet, the terms on which women are incorporated and accepted into local society and the negotiation of cultural difference within unequal structural positions happens in diverse ways often varying in accordance with women's prior standing and cultural background. Thus, many Kerala women, who generally tend to be more educated and capable of financial independence, can negotiate much better terms for themselves in the marriage than the poor, uneducated women from Bihar or Bengal.

In marrying, women have to adjust to a radically different and far more patriarchal culture. Beginning with differences in food, clothing and language, women have to adapt to more symbolic cultural differences. The language of the Haryanvis is a dialect of Hindi while the women speak diverse languages such as Bengali, Malayalam, Assamese, and Marathi etc. Verbal communication is difficult, leaving the new bride socially and psychologically isolated. Haryanvis are mostly vegetarian while the women they are marrying are used to eating meat and fish. The women's cuisine is rice-based unlike in the North where it is wheat-based. The women have to adjust to a system where the separation of genders is radical, an expression of which is the local form of purdah called 'ghunghat', a veil for the face. Hindu women outside of the North do not observe purdah and have easier interaction with members of the opposite sex and with members of older generations. Freedom of mobility in their natal homes is far greater. Carrying out all tasks while keeping the face veiled is felt unnaturally constraining. In women's narratives, learning to make 'chapattis' (griddle cooked unleavened bread) is a symbol of the tough adjustment they have to make. They are scolded or beaten until they learn to make good chapattis even as they are deprived of their own food. But, more than the physical adjustment and learning new work tasks, it is the distancing from one's own culture and the literal disowning of it that strikes at the soul. The body of the woman itself becomes written upon, in its transformation into a Haryanvi body. Over time, the women become perfect speakers of the local language and dialect and their dress and demeanour changes. Rites and rituals of their own land are replaced by that of the husband's; a cultural forgetting takes place, being re-awakened only when they encounter others from their own culture. The birth of children ties them down to their new home as it is through children that they acquire a stake in the husband's home and property and a right to continue to live where they have invested their labour, productive and reproductive.

Given the enormous distance from their natal homes and the expense of travelling, women who married in the 1980s did not keep much contact with their families. In more recent marriages, with the improvement in communications, women are able to keep in touch and visit occasionally. Yet, this does not substitute for kind of support networks that a local bride may have with her natal home and relatives. Women attempt to build their own 'community' by bringing sisters, relatives and neighbours from their villages to enter marriages with local men. In the process, some of them become 'agents' or matchmakers, making small profits for themselves.

As the marriage squeeze becoming tighter, the trickle of women which can be documented from the eastern states of Assam and Bengal from the 1980s onwards has literally turned into a flood. At present, the number of women migrating for marriage into Haryana and the number of men seeking brides from various parts of the country has escalated enormously. Earlier marriages of cross-region women were mostly with widowers and older men—those who couldn't find local brides. The age gap between the spouses was large and most couples were illiterate or semiliterate. (Kaur: 2004). In more recent cases, the couples are closer in age, the men are younger, couples are more educated and for many males this is their first marriage. It is obvious that men are anticipating that a local bride will be hard to come by and are taking steps earlier than in the past to acquire a cross-region bride.

In some ways, both the men and women who are forced to seek marriage outside their cultural universe are marginalized within their own societies. While poverty is a central factor among the women, sometimes abusive first marriages drive them out. At other times, as in the case of the Kerala women who are more literate and independent, it is factors such as lack of success in matching horoscopes for marriage or demand for gold by the prospective in-laws which leads them to becoming 'over-age' while they wait for proposals. Most women who marry out are from poor families from poor states. They often come from families of several sisters and may not have a living father or brother who would have been responsible for arranging their marriage. Some parents find it difficult to arrange their daughters' marriages if they have to fulfil unrealistic dowry demands. As non-marriage of daughters compromises family honour, parents are happy to marry their daughters to men who do not ask for any dowry and who pay for all marriage expenses. Matchmakers convince parents that the grooms come from more prosperous areas of India and that their daughters will be happy. Often the women think the same.

Men who marry out are generally those who have little or no land, no employment or lack education, are physically handicapped or tinged by social scandal. Widowers seeking second wives have to look beyond Haryana. Few men over the age of thirty-five can find a local bride. Thus, men who are lower down in the social hierarchy in some way or the other suffer. Yet, the increasing complexity of the situation as it unfolds is pointed to by two facts—that much younger men are now marrying out and that women from non-poor states are also entering such marriages. Political economy, gender dynamics and local rules of marriage in both bride-sending areas and bride-receiving areas need to be important elements in the explanation.

Although, demography and local culture may be responsible for initiating an initial marriage or two, these often turn into dense networks between states and even between specific villages. As the 'bride-trade' becomes more lucrative, besides women who become match-makers, men have begun to enter the arena. Although there may be an element of trafficking (introduced with the entry of men) in some transactions, most marriages are monogamous and remain stable. While men may view the transaction as 'buying a bride' because of the sum expended on travel, rituals and payment to the matchmaker, women's parents do not receive any money and do not see it as having 'sold' their daughter. In some cases, unscrupulous relatives sell girls in marriage, but this is most often not the case.

Conclusion

Many scholars have speculated whether such marriages which cut across boundaries of caste, region and sometimes even religion and in addition are dowry-less will have some positive consequences. Will they be able to challenge and break down the rigidities of caste, region and dowry? The jury is out on many of these questions as the situation is still an evolving one. A lot will depend on the influence women in cross-region marriages are able to have in their marital homes. The manner of their and their children's integration into local society would be crucial. Will the scarcity of local women and of brides raise the value of girl children and of women in these areas? Will it turn the sex ratio around? There are fears and some evidence that since women will be in short supply, they will be subjected to higher levels of violence. The value of local women may go up in the local marriage market but they will be at risk in various other ways. And women who have entered marriages far away from home and are cultural strangers may end up being treated as second class citizens for long.

(Ravinder Kaur is with the Department of Humanities and Social Sciences, Indian Institute of Technology, New Delhi. She can be reached at ravinder.iitd@gmail.com).

References

Agnihotri, Satish (2000) Sex Ratio Patterns in the Indian Population: A Fresh Exploration. New Delhi: Sage Publications.

Attané, I. and C. Z. Guilmoto, eds. (2007) Watering the Neighbour's Garden: The Growing Demographic Female Deficit in Asia. Paris: CICRED.

Berreman, G.D. (1993) Himalayan Polyandry and the Domestic Cycle, in, Uberoi, P. (ed.) Family, Kinship and Marriage in India. Delhi: Oxford University Press.

Bhatt, P.N. Mari and Shiva S.Halli (1999) "Demography of Brideprice and Dowry: Causes and Consequences of the Indian Marriage Squeeze" *Population Studies*, Vol. 53, No.2 pp 129-148.

Bourdieu, Pierre (1977) Outline of a Theory of Practice. Cambridge: Cambridge University Press.

Bose, Ashish (2001) India's Billion Plus People. Delhi: B.R. Publishing Company.

Chowdhry, Prem (1994) The Veiled Women. New Delhi: Oxford University Press.

Chowdhry, Prem (2007) Contentious Marriages, Eloping Couples. New Delhi: Oxford University Press.

Croll, Elizabeth. (2000) Endangered Daughters. London and New York: Routledge.

DasGupta, and Li Shuzhuo (1999) "Gender Bias in China, South Korea and India 1920-1990: Effects of War, Famine and Fertility Decline", in *Development and Change* Special Issue in Gender, Poverty and Well-being, Vol. 30, No.3, July, pp 619-52.

DasGupta, Monica (1987) "Selective Discrimination against Female Children in Rural Punjab, India", *Population and Development Review,* Vol. 13, No.1, pp 77-100.

DasGupta, Monica (1995) "Fertility decline in Punjab, India: Parallels with Historical Europe, *Population Studies: A Journal of Demography*, 49, pp 481-500.

Hershman, Paul (1981) Punjabi Kinship and Marriage. Delhi: Hindustan Publishing Corporation.

Jeffery, Roger and Patricia Jeffery (1997) Population, Gender and Politics, Cambridge: Cambridge University Press.

Jha, P., Kumar R., Vasa, P., et al 2006 "Low Male to Female Sex Ratio of Children Born in India: National survey of 1.1 million households in *The Lancet* (online) available at *www.thelancet.com.*

Kaur, Ravinder (2004) "Across-Region Marriages: Poverty, Female Migration and the Sex Ratio", *Economic and Political Weekly,* Vol. 39, No.25 June 19-25, 2595-2603.

Kaur Ravinder (2007) "Declining Juvenile Sex Ratios: Economy, Society and Technology. Explanations from Field Evidence", *Margin – The Journal of Applied Economic Research* 1:2(2007) 231-245, Sage Publications, Los Angeles/London/New Delhi/Singapore.

Patel, Tulsi, ed. (2007) Sex Selective Abortion in India. New Delhi: Sage Publications.

Pettigrew, Joyce (1979) Robber Noblemen: A Study of the Political System of the Sikh Jats. London: Routledge and Kegan Paul.

Sen, Amartya (1990) "More than 100 million women are missing" in *The New York Review of Book,* Volume 37, No.20, 1990.

11

Kinship System, Fertility and Son Preference among the Muslims: A Review

Rosina Nasir and A K Kalla

This review illustrates the differences in kinship system between north (by large patrilineal) and south (by large matrilineal) India—it is an important factor to bring about regional disparities in sex preference of children by the Hindu parents but not by the Muslim parents in whom kinship system is traditionally unique, as it shares similarity with the Dravidian system in the marriage pattern and inheritance from paternal side and similarity in kinship terminology with Indo Aryan system of the north, while among the Hindus, it is traditionally based on patrilineal inheritance, not withstanding the Hindu succession Act of 1956. Though dowry and sex selective abortion are the determinants of status of women among the Hindus, they are generally not practiced among the Muslims. However, the lower education status, economic status and social status (due to patriarchy and religious ideologies) respectively, together produce circumstances leading to son being seen as the best socio-economic insurance

by the Muslim women. This review of studies conducted on the above topic shows that, high fertility among the Muslim women is also a consequence of son preference arising out of socio-economic compulsion in the traditional absence (due to strict religious prohibition) of sex selective abortions.

Introduction

India attracts attention of the world because of gender bias—the small number of females as compared to males as a demographic feature. This feature is mainly attributed to Hindus who comprise over three-quarters of the Indian population. Although the concern over India's imbalanced sex-ratio is not new, India's deficit of females was first cited in 1901, the sex-ratio for all of India (female/1000 male) was 972, in 1971 the ratio further declined to 930 and after a small climb in 1981 to 936 the ratio in 1991 was 929, now it has raised again to 933 in 2001. According to the 'First Report on Religion Data, 2001' released by the Registrar General and Census Commissioner of India. The child sex-ratio of Muslim (950/1000) is better than that of Hindus (925/1000), despite the fact that the over all literacy rates among Hindus (65.1%) is higher than that of Muslim (59.1%) populations. The data presented in Table 1 shows a large difference in child sex-ratios between Hindu and Muslim populations both in the rural and urban areas. Further, it was listed in the Census of India, 2001, that sex selective abortion is one of the reasons for the declining sex-ratio of the child population (age group, 0-6yrs) and it can be concluded from the data that the problem of sex selective abortion is predominant in the Hindu community. In order to understand the abuse of technology to abort female foetuses, one needs to understand the wider social historical context of gender bias on the population. It is needed to take into account the socio-economic, cultural and ideological factors that contribute to the neglect and murder of females beyond the foetal stage.

Another important factor, which needs to be highlighted, is the continuing bias shown by prosperous communities towards the girl child. Census 2001 listed that the Sikh community with 786 girls for every 1,000 boys has the lowest child sex-ratio followed by the Jains (870/1000). This fact is found to be corroborated by Agnihotri (2000) findings that, female status is not necessarily correlated with the higher family income meaning that, the wealthy not only raise the standard for the poor classes to emulate, but also suffer from the same pressure to have sons who will bring in wealth, maintain their honour and facilitate their ability to meet increased financial expectations. In addition to this, Agnihotri (2000) suggests that, instituting social programs to increase female labour participation (a factor found to increase women's status and empowerment) is virtually meaningless when applied to the wealthier classes who may not want or need their women to be assimilated into the job market. Hence, from the above, it can be concluded that indicators like educational status and economic status are not considerable enough to influence sex-ratio and women's status.

Table1: Sex Ratio – Rural and Urban Children (F/M Age Group 0-6) Among Hindus and Muslims, India, 2001

Areas	Hindus	Muslims
Rural	931	955
Urban	898	937
Total	925	950

Source: 'The First Report on Religion Data', Census of India 2001, Registrar General and Census Commissioner, India.

So, which are the features we have to look into to understand the skewed sex-ratio of India? Is it cultural variations or regional variations or religious variations which affect the sex-ratio? Why a son is so much more preferred in Indian culture? Is it true for all regions and all religions in India? In this respect, we would like to mention that having a girl and then wanting a boy is a universal phenomenon occurring in any society (Grant, 1998). But it must not necessarily be at the cost of females' death. Grant (1998) mentions that in western cultures, there is an overall pattern which remains persistently son—preferring. However, these cultures do not have low sex-ratio (male/female) like India (1.07) or China (1.06) (CIA-The World Fact Book, 2001).

Influence of Variation in Kinship System and Culture on Sex-Ratio

Son is preferred in the Indian context because, sons are considered to contribute to the family's resources and family name is preserved through a son; sons are expected to carry out certain ceremonial death rites and sons and not daughters are expected to contribute towards parents in their old age. As far as regional variation is concerned, the distinct sex-ratio divide between the north-western and south-eastern region of the Indian subcontinent (Miller, 1984), is part of a wider cultural division recognized as the Indo-Aryan (north)-Dravidian (south) divide. Relevant features of the Indo-Aryan kinship systems, identified by Dyson and Moore (1983: 43-45) are: spatially exogamous marriage rules; social co-operation between males based on descent; exclusion of women from property inheritance chain. These contrast with the features of the southern kinship system namely, spatially endogamous marriages, equal importance of affinity and descent in social co-operation among males and inclusion of women in the property inheritance processes. In the Indo-Aryan system, the bride-givers are accorded an inferior status as compared to those who receive the bride; this can be envisaged in marriage rituals like washing of the feet of the groom's parents by certain person(s) from the bride's side. Thus, it is one of the many reasons why reciprocal marriage is forbidden in the Indo-Aryan system where, women have been assigned a lower status compared to the Dravidian system. These cultural disparities show that, the south tends to be more female-friendly and women in this area tend to be less subordinate to men. Another important aspect of the southern kinship system is matrilineal kinship system and daughters, like sons, can and do render old-age support to their parents.

Rules of marriage may also be responsible for the distorted sex-ratios, in the south, cross-cousin marriages are predominant; there is less social and geographical distance between the bride-giver and the bride-taker; lineages are perpetuated rather than reconfigured as in the north, where a new bride is viewed with suspicion and restraint, coming from distant villages, resulting in elated social status and social value of females in the south, which in turn may influence sex-ratio.

This seems to be corroborated by Das Gupta's (1987) study which draws a connection between inheritance pattern and sex-ratios. Gopalakrishna Kumar (1989) also emphasizes the importance of exploring the influence of women's political and economic power to regional variations in sex-ratios. These findings are evident in case of Kerala, which has historically shown positive sex-ratio. However, it also has characteristics that suggest better gender equity: it has generally had the lowest fertility rates, the highest level of female literacy, a high age at marriage and fairly good receptivity to contraception. Kumar (1989) also points to the preponderance of matrilineal inheritance as a possible explanatory reason for both the positive sex-ratio and the greater gender equity that has set Kerala apart. While in the north, Chandigarh, capital of Punjab, has the lowest sex-ratio i.e., 773 (Provisional Population Totals: India. Census of India 2001, Paper 1 of 2001). Das Gupta (1987) emphasized that, patrilineal descent is a key organizing principle of the Jat Kinship system (the dominant group in Punjab are the Jats, a land owning caste, in whom, son is given more preference over daughter). Further added that cultural practices may contribute to low sex-ratio in Punjab. He stated:

> "There is no question of women owning land. If she insists on her right to inherit land equally under the civil law, she would stand a good chance of being murdered".

Like Das Gupta (1987), Nag (1991) also had given a descriptive account of son preference and its regional differences in India—a strong son preference in northern states compared to the southern, reflecting difference in Kinship structure, female autonomy and other social characteristics.

The resource flow is always from the woman's father to the man's family in the form of dowry at the time of marriage and even after the initial payment of dowry which has been given as a reason for exclusion of women from inheritance in Hindus. However, the Hindu succession Act, 1956, has been introduced giving equal right of inheritance to the daughter along with the son. But, it hoists a question as to how far that condemnation of dowry system coupled with advocacy of reforms of the daughter's rights as a heir to the property of her natal family solves the problem of aversion against female child. How far the law is being enforced or is it able to cause any change in attitude towards female in Hindu patrilineal society, where daughters are considered transitory members in their natal family and their position depends on the number of sons they produce?

From a close examination of Kerala and Punjab, it appears that in both the states, in spite of the higher literacy rate and low fertility rate, wide gap keeps going in sex-ratios due to variation in the law of inheritance, dowry system, rules of marriage and females' place of residence after marriage which affect female status and in turn results in disturbed sex-ratios.

Influence of Religion on Fertility Behaviours and Sex-ratio

After the above views on variations as a result of regions, next crucial aspect, which needs to be investigated, is, do religious beliefs have something to do with sex-ratios? Does son preference exist in all religions or differ from one religion to another? Is declining sex-ratio an indicator of low status of women, if it is, then, how far is it true for different religions? Keeping these questions in mind, in this section, difference in the sex-ratios in people of two different religions, namely, Hindus and Muslims has been discussed. In this section, women's status among Muslims concerning law of inheritance, rules of marriage and kinship system will be scrutinized, keeping in retrospect the Hindus.

Cain's (1979, 1982) work based largely in rural Bangladesh suggests that, in the patriarchal environment which restricts the movements and the range of activities of women, effectively eliminating opportunities for employment and then by fostering both economic and social dependence of women upon men "*....the best risk insurance for women .... is to produce sons, as many and as soon as possible*" (Cain, 1979).

Sex preference can be a constraint on fertility decline, if couples who have already reached their desired family size continue childbearing until they achieve the desired sex composition of children (Nag, 1991). Sheps (1963) has shown mathematically that, if the probability of having a boy is the same for all individuals, the expected family size increases with increasing preference for one sex over the other. For example, in a hypothetical situation of perfect fertility control, if all fertile couples desire of minimum of two sons and would stop childbearing after having two, they would average 3.88 children, whereas, if all couples desire at least one son and one daughter, they would average 3.00 children.

Census 2001 listed that Muslim child sex-ratio is higher than that of Hindus in spite of its low female literacy and low economic status. A demographic feature like infant mortality among Muslims, at 59 per 1000, is much lower than that among Hindus, at 77 per 1000 (Bhat, 2003) and child mortality, which is 83 per 1000 for Muslims, substantially lower than child mortality among Hindus at 107 per 1000 (IIPS and ORC Marco International, 2000). Bhat (2003) study on child mortality and Census 2001 on child sex-ratio are evident to show Muslims are less averse to daughters than Hindus. But this does not deny the existence of son preference attitude.

This greater sex-ratio somewhere intends to probe the long existing speculation on the inferior status of women among Muslims as compared to Hindus. Also, the question whether this improved sex-ratio is a consequence of no son preference or of higher status of women among Muslims needs proper inspection. Further, it is needed to look into, cultural practices within Islam in this respect; how are they different from the Hindu system and to what extent non-Muslim communities (especially Hindus) affect the social life of the Muslims. It needs to be emphasized here that the prohibition of abortion in the holy book, Q'uran, is one of the many reasons for the sex-ratio going in favour of Muslim girls.

Apart from this, household dynamics about the values of females and sex-ratios provides the important insight for differential mortality rates by sex. Chen (1982), D'Souza and Chen (1980) and Chen *et al.,* (1981) study on rural Bangladesh investigate the reason for decline in differential mortality by sex. D'Souza and Chen (1980) point out that son preference in parental care, feeding patterns, intra family food distribution and treatment of illness favoring males, are the possible causes of the differences in child mortality rates. Chen *et al.,* (1981) provide important evidence of the social mechanisms manifest differential access to health and nutrition by sex preference. They found that differential allocation of food result in disparities in nutritional status with respect to sex and male children brought to the hospital more frequently than female children.

Further, it is reasonable to add here, that unlike Hindus, the cultural practice of payment of high dowry is not explicit among Muslims. It is taken as gifts to the bride by her family member but is not obligatory and not demanded. In this respect, Chaudhry (1982) mentioned that:

> "In India, Bangladesh and Morrocco, the net negative reward from having a daughter (because of dowry system) is in fact so great that, parents are not motivated to have additional children after a string of prior daughters

since their chance of having a son with next birth is only slightly greater than 50 per cent. In Taiwan, on the other hand, where couples with prior daughters are more likely to have another birth than couples with prior sons, it does not appear that the net negative reward for another daughter is as large as the net positive reward for another son (dowry is not a major issue in Taiwan)".

Thus, two inferences can be made from his study, first that son preference is a universal phenomenon in every society and second, dowry is the major cause for females facing neglect earlier, when sex selective technology was not available and later, of female foeticide in the techno savvy era in India.

Religious teachings play a major role, as Muslims translated prescribed Islamic tenets into practice, in which, dowry system is not engendered and abortion is strictly forbidden. This acts as the safeguard against sex selective abortion. But one important point that needs to be examined is the impact of socio-cultural milieu, as Muslims form the integral part of a wider complex.

It would be worth mentioning at this juncture that the Muslim kinship system is unique. It shares similarities with Dravidian system of south in terms of law of inheritance considering women, recognizing the distinction between cross and parallel consanguineal relatives and giving preference to consanguineous marriage apart from uncle-niece marriage and on the other hand, Muslims society is patriarchal and patrilineal in nature and follow kin terminological framework similar to Indo-Aryan Kinship system. By and large, it is found that, Muslim women gain respect and status when they marry and have children, thereby improving their bargaining position in the social structure (Youseef, 1978). Maulana Ashraf Ali Thanavi, in the early 20th century wrote in a compendium that bless a Muslim women by wishing her husband, brother or children long life or wishing for her many sons and grandsons (Minault, 1998: 62). So, son preference is an inevitable phenomenon even in the Muslim community.

According to Islamic law of inheritance, a son receives twice as much as a daughter, a brother twice as much as a sister and a husband twice as much as a wife. Besides this, Islam considers dower (*mehr*) and maintenance being compulsory on the part of the husband. It reduces women's financial commitments and increases man's burden proportionately; bearing this extra burden on man in mind, his share in inheritance has been fixed at twice that of women. From this, it can be assumed that the high frequency of consanguineous marriages is a consequence to retain the family property which is entitled to the girls. Thus, consanguineous marriage, law of inheritance, compulsion on dower and less importance to dowry among Muslims, promote the social environment to foster female birth and less aversion towards them. Nonetheless, a more deep-seated subject of inquiry is how many girls do get their share of property even when they seek for it? Is the amount of dower adequate enough to support her or just a ritual or custom to perform? How far is it true that acceptance of the dowry system which is the major force behind son preference among Hindus is completely absent in Muslims, as all religions equally tend to be affected by the process of 'Sanskritatization' (Srinivas, 1962)—the adoption of the ritual of higher castes.

All these questions to some extent are answered by Mistry's (2001) study on Muslims of Malegaon. Her study reported that the customs of dowry is not prevalent among Malegaon Muslims. Dower (*Mehr*) though theoretically an institution to empower Muslim women, but in practice, it has failed to do so. It is observed that, dower amount is too meager which makes it merely an economic right on paper. Her study indicated, high frequency of non-consanguineous marriages and absence of preference for son among them. Regarding property rights, 61 per cent of the women's parents, husband or relatives had no property to inherit and only 4 per cent of the women get a share in property. It is concluded from her study that absence of dowry system and property to inherit clubbed with high frequency of non-consanguineous marriages are the major factors influencing the attitude of Muslim women of Malegaon for son preference.

It is, therefore, reasonable to suppose that Muslims' higher sex-ratio is not an outcome of elevated female status. Though in part, Muslims' kinship pattern is similar to Dravidian kinship system, it is not reinforced by high female literacy rate unlike in southern states. However, there is no denying the fact that, Muslims show a much lower degree of "daughter aversion" than the Hindus, and this provides a plausible explanation for their larger families (Iyer, 2004).

The second feature is that, fertility rate of Muslims women is remarkably higher than that of their Hindu counterparts. National family Health Survey (NFHS), conducted in 1998-99 shows that, the total fertility rate for Hindus is 2.8 and for Muslims it is 3.6, (International Institute for Population Sciences and ORC Marco International, 2000). "Particularized theology" argument has been that it is the very essence of religion that influences fertility, irrespective of any socio-economic or demographic factors. Higher fertility of Indian Muslims is blamed as a result of their adherence to the tenets of Islam in a more orthodox manner and their opposition to family planning programs. Although Islam gives permission for using birth control measures on several grounds, one of them being husband's incapability to bring up more children.

Fertility Rates 1950-55 to 1995-2000, Estimates for 2003

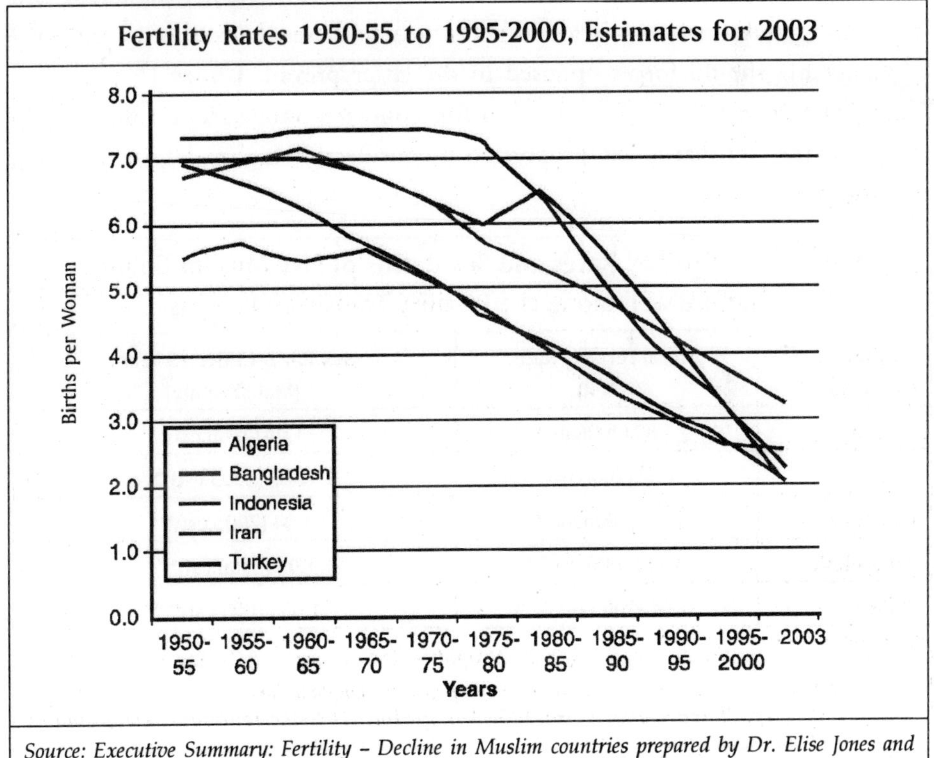

Source: Executive Summary: Fertility – Decline in Muslim countries prepared by Dr. Elise Jones and reviewed by Dr. Charles F. Westoff in July 2003.

However, Saw's (1989) study emphasized that Malay population of Singapore stands out as the first Muslim population in the world to have achieved replacement level fertility. Similarly Iran, an Islamic nation has shown phenomenal decline in fertility, dropping from 5.5 in 1988 to below 2.8 in 1996, more than a 50 percent decline in 6 years. The figure for the year 2000 is 2.17 according to Iran Demographic and Health Survey, 2000. Abbasi-Shavazi suggested the social and cultural context of the society along with certain government policies such as rural development, health improvement, and the rise of literacy paved the way for a successful family planning program introduced by the Islamic government. It is striking that, fertility has fallen farthest and fastest in Iran which is ruled by clerics and in Algeria where Islamic fundamentalism is also very strong (see graph). Indonesia and Bangladesh are large Muslim dominated Asian countries with appreciable non-Muslim minorities, have shown decline in total fertility rates (see graph). Total fertility rates of Indonesia and Bangladesh are 2.44 (2005 est.) and 3.11 (2006 est.) respectively. In Turkey, Bangladesh and Indonesia, family planning is identified largely with secular authority and may be vulnerable should forces opposed to the latter prevail. Under 15 years sex-ratios (Male/Female) of these five Muslim countries range from 1.04 to 1.06 indicating the fact that males' proportion is considerably higher despite declining fertility rates. (Table 2)

Table 2: Total Fertility Rates and Sex Ratios of Five Muslim Countries that are well along the Fertility Transition Process

Muslim countries	Total Fertility Rate (TFR)	Sex Ratio Under 15 Years (Male/Female)
Algeria	1.89 (2006.est)*	1.04 (2006.est)*
Iran	1.82 (2005.est)**	1.06 (2005.est)**
Indonesia	2.44 (2005.est)***	1.04 (2005.est)***
Bangladesh	3.11 (2006.est)****	1.05 (2006.est)****
Turkey	1.94 (2005.est)*****	1.05 (2005.est)*****

Sources: *****<*http://fixedreference.org/2006-Wikipedia-CD-Selection/wp/t/Turkey.htm*>

****<*http://en.wikipedia.org/wiki/Demographics_of_Bangladesh*>

***<*http://fixedreference.org/2006-Wikipedia-CD-Selection/wp/dDemographics_of_Indonesia.htm*>

**<*http://www.answers.com/topic/demographics-of-iran*>

*<*http://en.wikipedia.org/wiki/Demographics_of_Algeria*>

Thus there is no simple relationship between Islam and fertility behaviour. But, increased under 15 years male proportion put forth that, whether this increased sex-ratio in demographically advanced Muslims is a natural phenomenon or an outcome of some of the sex preference keeping in mind that abortion is forbidden by Q'uran.

Iyer (2004) shows that, Muslims of India though having evidence of higher fertility, also display lower degrees of girl child aversion. It has been noticed that, the increase in the likelihood of Muslim women terminating their fertility after the birth of a son or daughter is substantially lower than the corresponding values for Hindus. So, it has been identified that Muslims treat their daughters better on account of significantly lower level of daughter aversion. He further emphasized that the reason for the higher fertility of Muslim women in relation to Hindu women may lie in daughters being more welcome in Muslims than in Hindu families. But here, it is more likely to address whether the increased sex-ratio in Muslims indicating a rise in fertility rate be an outcome of son preference or is it a sign of welcome for a daughter in a family, despite the fact that female literacy is low in Muslims. Daughter aversion does not imply to only sex selective abortion, but also neglect, low education, low exposure to outer world and less freedom which needs to be considered as attitudinal aversion which suppress women's development and lead to lower status of women in society. Thus, it is required to carry out holistic study keeping in perspective variables like social status, nutritional status, economic status, and educational status, access to health facilities, decision-making ability and religious ideologies, facilitate to throw light on reasons for differences in differential frequency of sex preference concerning religion.

(Rosina Nasir and A K Kalla, Department of Anthropology, University of Delhi, Delhi 110 007, India. They can be reached at roseena_nasir@yahoo.com and akkalla@rediffmail.com).

References

Abbasi-Shavazi, Mohammad, Jalal: Recent changes and the future of fertility in Iran. *http: //www.un.org/esa/population/publications/completingfertility/ 2RevisedABBASIpaper.PDF* (Retrieved August 10, 2006).

Agnihotri, S.D.: *Sex-ratio Patters in the Indian Population: A Fresh Exploration.* Sage Publications, New Delhi (2000).

Bhat, M. and Zavier, F.: Fertility decline and gender bias in Northern India. *Demography,* 40(4): 637-657 (2003).

Cain, M., Khanam, S.R. and Nahar, S.: Class, patriarchy, and women's work in Bangladesh. *Population and Developmental Review,* 5(3): 433 (1979).

Cain, M.: Perspectives on Family and Fertility in Developing countries. *Population Studies,* 36(2): 159-175 (1982).

Cain, M.: Women's status and fertility in Developing countries: Son Preference and Economic security.

Center for policy studies working paper No.110. The Population Council, New York (1984).

Census 2001. From *http://www.cyberjournalist.org.in/census/censex0.html* (Retrieved July 26, 2006)

Census of India: *First Report on Religion Data, 2001.* Registrar General and Census Commissioner, India. (2001)

Chaudhary, R. H.: *Social Aspects of Fertility: With Special Reference to Developing Countries.* Vikas Publications, New Delhi (1982).

Chen, L., Huq, E. and D'Souza, S.: Sex bias in the family: Allocation of Food and health care in rural Bangladesh. *Population and Development Review,* 7(1): 54-70 (1981).

Chen, L.: Where have the women gone? Insights from Bangladesh on the low sex-ratio of India's population. *Economic and Political, Weekly,* March 6, 1982, p. 364-372 (1982).

CIA: The World Fact Book (2001) *http://www.umsl.edu/services/govdocs/wofact2001/index.html* (Retrieved August 10, 2006)

Das, G.M.: Selective discrimination against female children in rural Punjab, India. *Population and Development Review,* 13(1): 90-95 (1987).

D'Souza, S. and Chen, L.: Sex differentials in mortality in rural Bangladesh. *Population and Development Review,* 6(2): 257-270 (1980).

Dyson, T. and Moore, M.: On kinship structure, female autonomy and demographic behaviour in India. *Population and Development Report,* 9(1): 35-60 (1983).

Grant, V.J.: *Maternal Personality Evolution and the Sex-ratio: Do Mothers Control the Sex of the Infant?* Routledge, London and New York (1998).

Iyer, S. and Borooah, V.: Religion and fertility in India: The role of son preference and daughter aversion. Cambridge Working Papers in Economics. (2004) <*http: //www.econ.cam.ac.uk/dae/repec/cam/pdf/ cwpe0436.pdf*> (Retrieved August 10, 2006).

Iyer, S.: *Demography and Religion in India.* Oxford University Press, New Delhi (2002).

Kelly, N.U.: *Some Socio-Cultural Correlates of Indian Sex-ratio: Case Studies of Punjab and Kerala.* Ph.D. Thesis. University of Pennsylvania, Pennsylvania (1975).

Kumar, G.: Gender, differential mortality and development: The experience of Kerala, *Cambridge Journal of Economics,* 13(4): 517-554 (1989).

Miller, B.: *The Endangered Sex. The Neglect of Female Children in Rural India.* Cornell University Press, Ithaca, New York (1981).

Minault, G.: *Secluded Scholars: Women's Education and Muslim Social Reform in Colonial India.* Oxford University Press, Delhi (1998)

Mistry, M.B.: *Muslim Fertility in India: A Micro- study.* Institute of Objective Studies, New Delhi (2001).

Nag, M.: Sex preference in Bangladesh, India and Pakistan, and its effects on Fertility. *Demography India,* 20(2): 163-185 (1991).

Saw, S.H: Muslim fertility transition: The case of the Singapore Malays, *Asia-Pacific Population Journal,* 4(3): 31-40 (1989).

Sheps, M.: Effects on family size of preference. *Pakistan Development Review,* 21(4): 555-565 (1963).

Srinivas, M. N: *Caste in Modern India and Other Essays.* Media Promoters and Publishers Pvt. Ltd. Bombay (1962).

Youssef, M.H.: The status and fertility patterns of Muslims women. pp. 69-99, In: *Women in the Muslim World* Cambridge. L.Beck and N. Keddie (Eds.). Harvard University Press, Cambridge (1978).

12

Understanding Parental Gender Preferences in Advanced Societies
Lessons from Sweden and Finland

Gunnar Anderson, Karsten Hank and Andres Vikat

Extending recent research on parental gender preferences in the Nordic countries, this study uses unique register data from Finland and Sweden (1971-1999) that provide us with the opportunity to compare childbearing dynamics and possible underlying sex preferences among native majorities and national minorities, namely, Finnish-born immigrants in Sweden and members of the Swedish-speaking minority in Finland. For Finland, we observe a continuous boy preference among the national majority and the Swedish-speaking minority as reflected in higher third-birth rates of mothers of two girls than of mothers of two boys. Evidence of similar preferences is found for Finnish-born migrants in Sweden where, the native-born population instead, appears to have developed a girl preference. In all cases, we also observe clear indications of a preference for having at least one child of each sex. Generally speaking, our findings support

Source: www.demographic-research.org/Volumes/Vol17/6/ Demographic Research: Volume 17, Article 6, October 2007.

an interpretation of parental gender preferences as a longstanding cultural phenomenon, related to childhood socialization rather than language group. Moreover, an analysis of regional and educational differentials in child-sex specific fertility behaviour in Sweden reveals no evidence, which supports various diffusion theories of persistence and change in parents' sex preferences for children.

1. Introduction

The desire for a son is the father of many daughters (Seidl 1995) it says—which is likely to explain much of the demographers longstanding interest in parental gender preferences. Attention for this topic has also been growing rapidly in recent studies on advanced western societies (e.g., Diekmann and Schmidheiny 2004; Hank and Kohler 2000; Lundberg 2005; Marleau and Saucier 2002; Raley and Bianchi 2006). This development might, first, be due to medical advances that facilitate parents' deliberate choice of their child's sex (e.g., Dahl *et al.,* 2003, 2006). Secondly, it has been argued that, in modern low-fertility societies, the influence of the sex composition of previous children on couples' childbearing behaviour might intensify because, factors affecting the decision to have another child should become more important (e.g., Gray and Evans 2005; Sloane and Lee 1983).

Most empirical evidence suggests an almost universally dominant pattern of parental sex preferences favouring at least one child of each sex (e.g., Arnold 1997; Hank and Kohler 2000). Although it has been claimed that changes in a society's gender system, may lead to a decreasing effect of children's sex on parents' fertility decisions (Pollard and Morgan 2002), recent studies have shown that modernization and increasing gender equality do not necessarily bring about parental gender indifference. The Nordic example (cf. Andersson *et al.,* 2006).[1] shows, that, on the one hand, new sex preferences (in favour of girls) are likely to have evolved in Denmark, Norway, and Sweden as recently as in the 1980s, while, on the other hand, culturally rooted preferences for sons in Finland have

1 See Brunborg (1987), Jacobsen *et al.,* (1999), Kartovaara (1999), and Schullström (1996) for earlier investigations of sex preferences for children and fertility decisions in the Nordic countries.

been left unaffected by improvements in women's social, political, and reproductive rights (see Dahl and Moretti, 2004, for related evidence from the US).

This article extends recent research by Andersson and colleagues (2006) in two ways. First, it proposes to improve our theoretical understanding of parental gender preferences in advanced societies and recent changes therein by accounting better for the possible role of social interaction, culture, and national institutions (Section 2). Second, it makes use of unique register data from Finland and Sweden for the period 1971-1999 (see Section 3), providing us with the opportunity to compare childbearing dynamics and sex preferences for children that may drive these among native majorities and national minorities, namely Finnish-born immigrants in Sweden and members of the Swedish-speaking minority in Finland (Section 4.1). The study is achieved by means of comparing differentials in parents' family building by the sex composition of their previous off-spring. Moreover, our Swedish data set allows us to investigate regional and educational differences in fertility behaviour and possible preferences of two-child mothers from 1981 onwards (Section 4.2). The concluding section connects our considerations and empirical findings (Section 5).

2. Theorizing Parental Gender Preferences

The Role of Social Interaction, Culture and Institutions

A major shortcoming of most studies investigating sex preferences is their relatively weak theoretical foundation, particularly, if they deal with more developed societies (e.g., Hank and Kohler 2003: Section II; see also Lundberg 2005). In this article, we suggest several basic mechanisms, through which sex preferences for children may be reproduced or changed. The first two are closely interrelated, namely: (1) social interaction and (2) culture. Another mechanism proposed here refers to (3) national institutions, particularly, such related to information and welfare-state systems (cf. Brockmann 2001; Andersson *et al.,* 2006).

The concept of social interaction can be fruitfully applied to the topic of our study, especially if we are trying to understand better, sudden changes in previously longstanding preferences (cf. Andersson *et al.,* 2006; Pollard and Morgan 2002). Social interaction may either serve as a channel for innovative interpersonal communication, facilitating the flow of information, or as conservative cultural forces, encouraging adherence to behavioural norms. Using the language of Montgomery and Casterline (1996), the former can be called social learning, while the latter can be described as social influence.

With regard to social learning, Bongaarts and Watkins (1996) distinguish the exchange of information and ideas on the one hand from the joint evaluation of their meaning in a particular context on the other hand. They suggest that social interaction processes take place at different levels of aggregation: "Just as personal networks connect individuals, so, channels of social interaction connect social and territorial communities within a nation and nations within the global society. Through these channels, actors at these three levels exchange and evaluate information and ideas and exert and receive social influence" (Bongaarts and Watkins 1996: 665).

Besides 'interpersonal communication', Montgomery and Casterline (1996: 154f.) explicitly account for those forms of social interaction, where "the information set is shaped by communications emanating from impersonal sources, such as the mass media, markets, and other aggregate social structures". There has been much debate about the influence of mass media on fertility (e.g., Westoff 1999; see also Stark and Kohler 2002), where modern means of communication are generally perceived to foster social change and to reduce, for example, regional differences in behaviour. This does not imply, though, that the evolution of new preferences or the continuation of traditional behaviour may not vary anymore between nations or across various subpopulations within a single country.

Different from the 'direct' transmission mechanism of social interaction, cultural normative patterns will rather be determined by individuals' internalization of basic normative attitudes and values at various stages during their life course. Hammel (1990: 475), for example, argues for "a view of culture that recognizes the agency of individuals in using behaviour as a symbol selected from a repertoire, that has some coherence and endures over time, but that is created and maintained by patterns of selection by actors as well as innovation". From this, Hammel (1990: 467) develops a notion of culture as "an intensely evaluative cloud of comments", where culture provides the normative and interpretative rules, according to which, individuals consider their fertility (and/or sex) preferences.

However, indivIduals may be subject to different contextual influences over time, and thus, individual behaviour can be influenced by lagged as well as by contemporaneous contextual effects (see, for example, Axinn and Yabiku 2001).

But more specifically: why should parents at all prefer having children of one sex, over having children of another sex? It is generally argued that children of a particular sex are desired to provide certain utilities, such as financial, social, or psychological benefits. In developing countries, for example, sons are presumed to have greater economic net utility than daughters, since male offspring is better able to provide assistance in agriculture and to serve as a simple social security system. In patrilineal societies, sons are also valued for continuing the family name. Daughters, on the other hand, should be more reliable in providing old age assistance. In addition, they are frequently desired to help with household tasks or to care for younger siblings. Thus, even in countries with a prevailing preference for sons, many families consider it important to have at least one daughter (e.g., Arnold 1997; Cleland *et al.*, 1983).

In industrialized societies children no longer provide economic net utility, but have rather become a source of significant time and monetary costs. However, Hoffman and Hoffman (1973) list a set of alternative values that parents may still attribute to their children, such as expansion of the self, affiliation, stimulation, accomplishment or social comparison (cf. Thomson 2001). At least with regard to some of these categories, different benefits may accrue from daughters or sons for each of the partners. Morgan *et al.*, (1988), for example, have argued that, boys might reduce parents' divorce risk, since fathers' attachments and obligations to their children and marital cohesion, are greater, if they have sons (see Diekmann and Schmidheiny, 2004, for a recent discussion of this father-involvement hypothesis). Women, on the other hand, may consider girls as easier to be raised or as more rewarding companions (e.g., Marleau and Saucier 2002). Since each partner might want to have a child of his or her own sex, couples may desire—and be better off with—a gender mix. This argument corresponds with empirical research on divorces in Sweden showing a slightly reduced divorce risk of two-child parents that have one child of each sex (cf. Andersson and Woldemicael 2001). Last but not the least, it has been shown that, parity matters a great deal, if parental gender preferences are considered. Results of a study analyzing values and disvalues attached to children in the Philippines, Korea, and the United States, for example, suggest that balancing of the family's sex composition is most important for family building, when the decision to have a third or a fourth child is considered, while general emotional and psychological rationales for having a child at all, dominate at lower parities (Bulatao 1981).

The role of institutions in changing sex preferences for children has been stressed by Pollard and Morgan (2002), who contend that more equal opportunities for women and men (induced by changes in the societal gender system) should result in a decreasing effect of children's sex on parents fertility decisions (see also Bongaarts 2001: 277). This argument, however, has not been left undisputed. Recent evidence from the Nordic countries (Andersson *et al.*, 2006) strongly suggests that modernization does not necessarily neutralize gender preferences, but that in some cases traditional values attached to sons may retain a foothold, while elsewhere, new sex preferences might evolve. Along the same lines, Brockmann (2001: 199) argues that, for example, increasing female labour-force participation and the growing burden of ageing should increase the value of a daughter, since she assumes both the role of a breadwinner and that of a caregiver. Moreover, changing expectations concerning the division of labour and family responsibilities between men and women (Bianchi *et al.*, 2000; Hank and Jürges 2007), followed by a more positive evaluation of women's role in society, might rather foster the development of a preference for girls (e.g., Hammer and McFerran 1988) than parental gender indifference, as proposed by Pollard and Morgan (2002).

Unfortunately, there is a huge gap between the fundamental significance of institutions, patterns of social interaction, and culture on the one hand and the empirical limitations to identify the nature of the underlying mechanisms, that are supposed to influence individual fertility preferences on the other hand. Observed outcomes in terms of family demographic behaviour and vital events can usually be generated by many different processes, but outcome data typically have only limited power to distinguish among alternative plausible hypotheses regarding these processes (cf. Manski 1995). Moreover, Axinn and Yabiku (2001: 1225) argue that, there may be independent effects of childhood and adult social contexts on adult decision-making: Social context during childhood, affects social organization in the child's family, which subsequently influences childbearing behaviour in adulthood. Mechanisms affecting the costs and benefits of childbearing, however, operate during adulthood as a person decides on childbearing. Mechanisms linked to the diffusion of [...] ideas may operate through either childhood or adult processes [...].

In this paper, we make an attempt to tackle some of the processes suggested to drive continuity and change in parental gender preferences, by comparing differentials in childbearing dynamics by the sex composition of existing children, among various population subgroups (national minority, regional, educational) in Sweden and Finland. Although some studies (e.g., Hank and Kohler 2003; Marleau and Saucier 2002) have shown that, sex preferences even for firstborn children may well exist in Western societies, we do not expect to find behaviourally relevant sex preferences among mothers of one child in any of the groups represented in our study, because, for those women the main consideration should merely be whether or when to have an additional child (see also Andersson *et al.*, 2006). With regard to potential differences we propose the following set of four hypotheses:

a. Assuming that long-standing cultural normative patterns—which the individual internalized during childhood and which thus continue to work independently of subsequent processes of social learning or social influence —matter, we hypothesize that Finnish-born migrants living in Sweden will tend to exhibit sex preferences similar to those of the non-migrant Finnish population. However, we may also find differences within the migrant population, namely between those who moved to Sweden early during childhood and those who migrated later during their life course. Because the former were regularly exposed to social interactions with Swedish peers before entering adulthood, they are likely to have 'learned' about fertility (and sex) preferences in the native population, possibly adopting these for themselves. This is unlikely to be the case (or only limited so) for 'late' adult migrants.

b. Considering the generally high degree of socio-demographic and socio-economic similarities (see below) and the sharing of the same national context during childhood and adulthood, we hypothesize that there will not be any substantial differences in parental gender differences between the Swedish-speaking minority and the majority population in Finland.

An alternative hypothesis, though, refers to the idea that the Swedish minority community—living in the Finnish coastal regions for centuries—may exert a relatively strong social influence on its members (cf. Finnäs 1997: 274). If different sex preferences were present historically, such influence could serve as a conservative cultural force, preserving these differences and preventing an equalization of behaviours. In addition, if innovations in social behaviour tend to follow linguistic barriers rather than national borders (cf. Watkins 1990), we would expect the Swedish-speaking minority to be more likely to pick up behaviours observed for the majority population of Sweden.

c. Because urbanites have often been suggested to act as forerunners of social change (e.g., Wirth 1938), we hypothesize that mothers living in the capital area of Sweden will tend to exhibit less 'traditional' gender preferences (potentially more often favoring daughters over sons) or develop any daughter preference observed for the general population earlier than their non-metropolitan counterparts.

d. Because education may be rendered an important determinant of attitudes towards women's role in society, one might assume a greater prevalence of modern preferences (potentially favouring daughters over sons) among the more highly educated[2]. More specifically, making again a diffusion argument, we hypothesize that any new girl preference in Sweden, developed earlier and/or more intensely among the more highly educated mothers than in the less educated population.

3. Study Populations, Data, and Method

In Finland, the Swedish-speaking minority has roots going back many centuries (for details see e.g., Finnäs 1997; 2003). When Finland was still part of the Swedish realm, Swedish was the dominant official language in government, business and culture. Today, Swedish and Finnish have an equal status as official languages. For example, in the educational system from elementary schools to universities, Swedish and Finnish language institutions exist in parallel. Similarly, a variety of Swedish mass media (television, radio, newspapers) is easily accessible.

2 Although recent evidence from Germany suggests a higher propensity of the more highly educated to favour daughters, the rare overall empirical evidence about the relationship between parents education and their sex preference for children remains unclear (cf. Hank & Kohler 2003).

About six percent of the Finnish population is Swedish-speaking, being geographically concentrated along the western and southern coastline. About half of the Swedish-speaking persons live in municipalities where they form the local majority. Another fifth of the Swedish minority lives in metropolitan areas, where their proportion of the total population is less than ten percent.

Although differences in socio-economic status and education between the Finnish-speaking majority and the Swedish-speaking minority are generally very small, the latter is still over-represented in white-collar occupations and under-represented among manual workers. Similarly, demographic behaviour generally differs more between regions in Finland than between language groups[3]. However, the Swedish-speaking minority is on retreat: during the 1950s and 1960s, substantial emigration to Sweden was observed, concurrent with a doubling of the Finnish-speaking population in the main Swedish settlement areas between 1950 and 1980. Also, since the mid-1970s, the number of linguistic intermarriages has outnumbered the unilingual Swedish ones.

In Sweden, immigrants from Finland comprise by far, the largest single foreign-born group (e.g., Svanberg and Runblom 1988). In addition to the shared history of the two nations, there are geographical and economic reasons for this. Finland, which is Sweden's nearest neighbour to the east, lagged behind economically, before finally catching up during the 1980s. This led to a large flow of labour migrants from Finland to Sweden, which was facilitated by the existence of a free Nordic labour market and slowed down only during the late 1970s to early 1980s, following the equalization in the living standards of the two countries. One result of the long intertwined migration history is that, many Finnish-born women have become partners of Swedish-born men. For a detailed description of fertility patterns of immigrant women in Sweden, see Andersson 2004; Andersson and Scott 2005; 2007.

Statistics on events to and characteristics of the native and foreign-born resident populations are collected and summarized by the Statistical Central Bureaus of Finland and Sweden, from whose population register systems the data for our

[3] See, however, Finnäs (1997) study on divorce. The author finds remarkably lower divorce rates among the Swedish-speaking minority than among the Finnish-speaking majority, suggesting that this might be a result of better social integration among the former group.

calculations are derived (cf. SCB 2003; Wallgren and Wallgren 2007). The population-registration systems have been computerized since the end of the 1960s and have a long history of full and reliable coverage of the local populations and their vital events. We use data on live births and the corresponding exposure times of risk for various subgroups of women—defined by parity, country of birth (Sweden), language group (Finland), region of residence (Sweden), and education (Sweden)—to calculate multivariate models of parity-specific birth risks by the sex composition of previous children. These occurrences and exposures are derived from the longitudinal information on the dates of each recorded birth of all women in Sweden and a 10% sample of women in Finland who were born in 1935 and 1937, respectively, and onwards. The data extracts that we have used include information on every such individual, who had ever been a resident in the respective countries in 1971-1999.

We estimate proportional-hazards models, whose results are presented as standardized relative risks of second and third births by the sex of the previous child or children for mothers in each of the two countries. The main explanatory variable is the sex of the previous child (for second births) or children (for third births). We regard any observable differences in parity-progression risks by that sex composition as a reflection of parents' gender preferences for children, assuming that, parents are more likely to continue childbearing, if they have not acquired their desired number and/or sex composition of children. We use calendar year (defined as a dummy variable depicting period effects in fertility by single calendar years) as another main variable of interest. By running an interaction between the sex of the previous child or children and calendar year, we aim to detect changes and continuities in parents' gender preferences for children. We present period trends in parity-progression risks for the years 1971-1999. We use age of mother (ranging from 15 to 44 years in seven age groups) and time since the previous birth (ranging from 0 to 10 years in six groups) as control variables in our analyses. All variables are treated as grouped categorical covariates. Table 1 provides basic descriptive statistics on our study populations of one- and two-child mothers in the two countries. They refer to mothers born and residing in Sweden and Finland respectively, as well as mothers born in Finland but residing in Sweden and Swedish-speaking mothers born and residing in Finland.

Table 1: Descriptive Statistics Study Populations of Finland and Sweden, 1971-99

	Woman-Years as One-Child Mother	Number of Second Births	Woman-Years as Two-Child Mother	Number of Third Births
Finland	373,800	57,000	436,900	22,100
Swedish minority in Finland	17,600	3,000	23,900	1,200
Sweden	4,996,500	900,100	7,112,800	343,300
Finnish-born migrants in Sweden	239,800	34,000	296,500	13,800

Source: Finnish and Swedish population registers, authors' calculations.

4. Results

4.1 Differences in Parental Sex Preferences Among National Majorities and Minorities in Finland and Sweden

Our first set of analyses compares childbearing dynamics among Finnish and Swedish native-born populations, members of the Swedish-speaking minority in Finland and Finnish-born immigrants in Sweden across the entire observation period 1971-1999, estimating separate models for one- and two-child mothers (see Table 2; also compare the results reported in Andersson *et al.*, 2006).

Table 2: Relative Risk of Giving Birth to Another Child for One- and Two-Child Mothers Respectively, in Finland and Sweden, 1971-99, by Sex Composition of Previous Children

	Finland	Swedish-Speaking Minority in Finland	Sweden	Finnish-Born Migrants in Sweden
Second-birth risks of mothers of:				
– one boy vs one girl	0.98	(0.95)	(1.00)	(0.99)
Third-birth risks of mothers of:				
– two girls vs one boy and one girl	1.28	1.23	1.21	1.24
– two boys vs one boy and one girl	1.17	(1.12)	1.27	1.18
– two boys vs two girls	0.92	(0.92)	1.05	0.95

Note: Effects that are not significant on a five-percent level are given in parentheses.

Source: Finnish and Swedish population registers, authors' calculations. Results are standardized for calendar year, age of mother, and time since previous birth.

A statistically significant association between the sex of the first child and second birth risk is observed only among the Finnish majority population, where the slightly lower risk (0.98)[4] of having another child after the birth of a son suggests a behaviourally relevant preference for boys. This finding is corroborated by the lower risk (0.92) of Finnish natives to experience a third birth after having had two boys (vs. having had two girls). Despite considerable fluctuations in the magnitude of these 'gendered' third birth intensities between single calendar years, Figure 1 depicts no systematic variations that would suggest changes in Finnish parents' son preference across time. Moreover, we detect a preference for a mixed composition of Finnish parents offspring, which is substantially stronger, though, if the firstborn children are both girls (1.28) rather than being two boys (1.17).

Figure 1: Relative Third-Birth Risks in Finland and Sweden, by Sex of the First Two Children, 1971-99 – Risks for Mothers of Two Boys Relative to Those of Mothers of Two Girls in Each Calendar Year

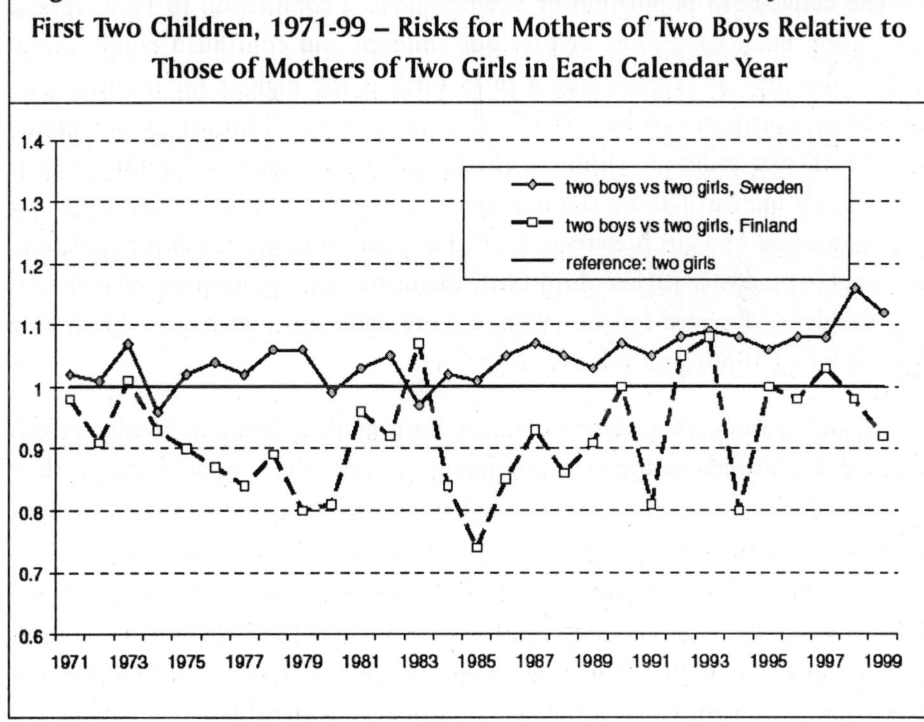

[4] A relative risk of 0.98 means that the second-birth intensity (for mothers of one boy) is two percent lower than that of mothers belonging to the reference category (mothers of one girl).

The Swedish-speaking minority in Finland exhibits a pattern similar to the one observed for the entire Finnish population, but the child-gender effect on continued childbearing is only statistically significant[5] at the five-percent level, when mothers of two girls are compared with mothers of one boy and one girl, where the former exhibit a 1.23 times higher risk of having another child.

Turning to Finnish-born migrants in Sweden, we also find that childbearing dynamics here do not differ from those observed in Finland. There is a clear evidence pointing to a son preference in this immigrant group: having two boys instead of two girls reduces the probability of having a third child (0.95); the strong preference for a mixed sex composition among one's offspring is gender biased, i.e., third birth intensities are the highest among mothers of two girls (1.24 vs. 1.18 among mothers of two boys).

The native-born population of Sweden shows a comparison to Finns reverse association between the sex of previous children and continued childbearing. The probability of experiencing a third birth is the highest for mothers who already gave birth to two boys (1.27 vs. mothers of mixed offspring) and among those with two same-sex children, the propensity to continue childbearing is significantly higher, if those children are male (1.05). In other words: there is a clear indication of a girl preference (at higher parities) in the Swedish population. Although, somewhat higher third-birth intensities among mothers of two sons can already be observed for the 1970s, a more stable girl preference evolved only from the mid-1980s onwards (see Figure 1).

Finally, an in-depth analysis of Finnish-born mothers living in Sweden reveals a significant difference between immigrant women who migrated during their childhood years (i.e., before age 15) and those who migrated as (young) adults; see Table 3. In the latter group, we find exactly the same association between the sex of previous children and continued childbearing that we observed for the Finnish non-migrant population. Mothers who migrated into the Swedish context earlier during their life-course, however, are characterized by a composition preference only, with no gender bias towards sons or daughters.

---

5 Note that the study population of a ten-percent sample of Swedish-speaking mothers in Finland is not much larger than that of any ordinary demographic sample-survey data.

Table 3: Relative Third-Birth Risk of Finnish-Born Mothers in Sweden, 1971-99, by Sex of the First Two Children for Women who Migrated to Sweden Before and After Age 15, Respectively

	Childhood Migration	Adult Migration
Third-birth risks of mothers of: – two girls vs one boy and one girl	1.18	1.28
– two boys vs one boy and one girl	1.19	1.18
– two boys vs two girls	(1.01)	0.92

Note: Effects that are not significant on a five-percent level are given in parentheses.

Source: Swedish population registers, authors calculations. Results are standardized for calendar year, age of mother, and time since second birth.

4.2 Regional and Educational Differences in Parental Sex Preferences Among the Native-born Population in Sweden

In addition to analyzing differences between 'national' majorities and 'ethnic' minorities, our Swedish data set also allows for analyses of regional and educational differences in childbearing dynamics in 1981-1999, as being related to parental gender preferences[6]. These analyses are based on socio-economic and demographic data for cohorts of women born in Sweden in 1945 onwards.

Accounting for information on whether the mother's residence is located in the capital area (Stockholm and its surrounding suburbs) or for example, in the forested Northern region of Norrland might substantiate speculations about the Finnish boy preference as being a result of persisting elements of some traditional thinking that attach a higher value to a son (cf. Andersson *et al.,* 2006). If this was the case, one might expect to find a weaker (if any) preference for daughters in the more remote areas of Northern Sweden than in the metropolitan area of Stockholm. However, Table 4 shows that there are no appreciable or systematic regional differences in parental gender preferences (indicated by differential third-birth intensities) between Stockholm, Norrland, and the rest of Sweden. Instead, we see in all regions an almost simultaneous emergence of girl preference from the mid-1980s, which intensified until the very end of our observation period.

6 Unfortunately, such detailed period analyses are not possible on the basis of our smaller sample of Finnish women. However, an inspection of parity-progression rates by educational level and sex of previous children (details not shown here) provides no evidence for differential gender preferences by educational group in Finland: The preference for having a boy appears equally strong for each educational category of Finnish mothers.

Table 4: Relative Third-Birth Risks in Sweden, by Sex-Composition of the First Two Children, 1981-99, for Women Residing in Different Regions of Sweden in Different Calendar-Year Periods

	1981-85	1986-90	1991-95	1996-99
Stockholm				
– two girls vs one boy and one girl	1.30	1.18	1.27	1.26
– two boys vs one boy and one girl	1.30	1.33	1.33	1.44
– two boys vs two girls	(1.00)	1.13	1.05	1.14
Norrland				
– two girls vs one boy and one girl	1.32	1.17	1.20	1.32
– two boys vs one boy and one girl	1.35	1.26	1.32	1.44
– two boys vs two girls	(1.02)	1.07	1.10	1.09
Rest of Sweden				
– two girls vs one boy and one girl	1.27	1.22	1.26	1.22
– two boys vs one boy and one girl	1.29	1.29	1.36	1.46
– two boys vs two girls	1.02	1.06	1.08	1.19

Note: Effects that are not significant on a five-percent level are given in parentheses.

Source: Swedish population registers, authors' calculations. Results are standardized for age and education of mother and time since second birth.

The 'new' girl preference observed in Sweden might possibly result from a growing share of more highly educated men and women, i.e., from changes in the population composition. Our investigation, however, does not reveal pronounced educational differentials in mothers' sex preferences (Table 5). Still, we observe evidence of a somewhat stronger preference for having a daughter—after having given birth to two boys—among women with secondary or post-secondary education, particularly so in the second half of the 1990s (see Figure 2). These educational differentials are not sufficiently strong, though, to support an argument that the more highly educated might have been pioneers of the emerging girl preference during the 1980s. On the contrary, Figure 2 rather suggests a striking similarity across educational groups in the timing of the emerging girl preference in Sweden.

Table 5: Relative Third-Birth Risks in Sweden, by Sex-Composition of the First Two Children, 1981-99, for Women at Different Educational Attainment in Different Calendar-Year Periods

	1981-85	1986-90	1991-95	1996-99
Mothers with primary education				
– two girls vs one boy and one girl	1.30	1.26	1.30	1.32
– two boys vs one boy and one girl	1.32	1.32	1.38	1.40
– two boys vs two girls	(1.01)	1.04	1.06	1.07
Mothers with secondary education				
– two girls vs one boy and one girl	1.29	1.19	1.27	1.28
– two boys vs one boy and one girl	1.35	1.29	1.38	1.51
– two boys vs two girls	1.05	1.08	1.08	1.18
Mothers with post-secondary education				
– two girls vs one boy and one girl	1.23	1.20	1.19	1.18
– two boys vs one boy and one girl	1.22	1.29	1.28	1.38
– two boys vs two girls	(0.99)	1.07	1.08	1.17

Note: Effects that are not significant on a five-percent level are given in parentheses.

Source: Swedish population registers, authors' calculations. Results are standardized for age and region of residence of mother and time since second birth.

5. Discussion

The research presented here aimed to improve our understanding of parental gender preferences in advanced societies, using Finland and Sweden as an example. Generally speaking, our main findings lend support to an interpretation of parental gender preferences as a longstanding cultural phenomenon, which may even persist in the presence of social and economic modernization (cf. Andersson *et al.,* 2006; Hank and Kohler 2000). This is suggested by the continuing apparent boy preference in Finland during the last decades of the twentieth century—both among the national majority and the Swedish-speaking minority—as well as by similar preferences among Finnish-born migrants in Sweden, where the native population tends to exhibit the opposite preference. That is, even in the absence of the social and institutional forces which may have contributed to shaping their fertility preferences in the Finnish mother country, these migrants have maintained their 'original' sex preferences and did not adopt those present in the Swedish context. However, if the event of migration already occurred during their childhood years, mothers

Figure 2: Relative Third-Birth Risks in Sweden, 1981-99, by Sex of the First Two Children for Women at Different Educational Attainments in Different Calendar-Year Periods. Risks for Mothers of Two Boys and Two Girls, Respectively, by Calendar Year, Relative to the Risk of a Mother of Two Girls in 1981 with Primary Education

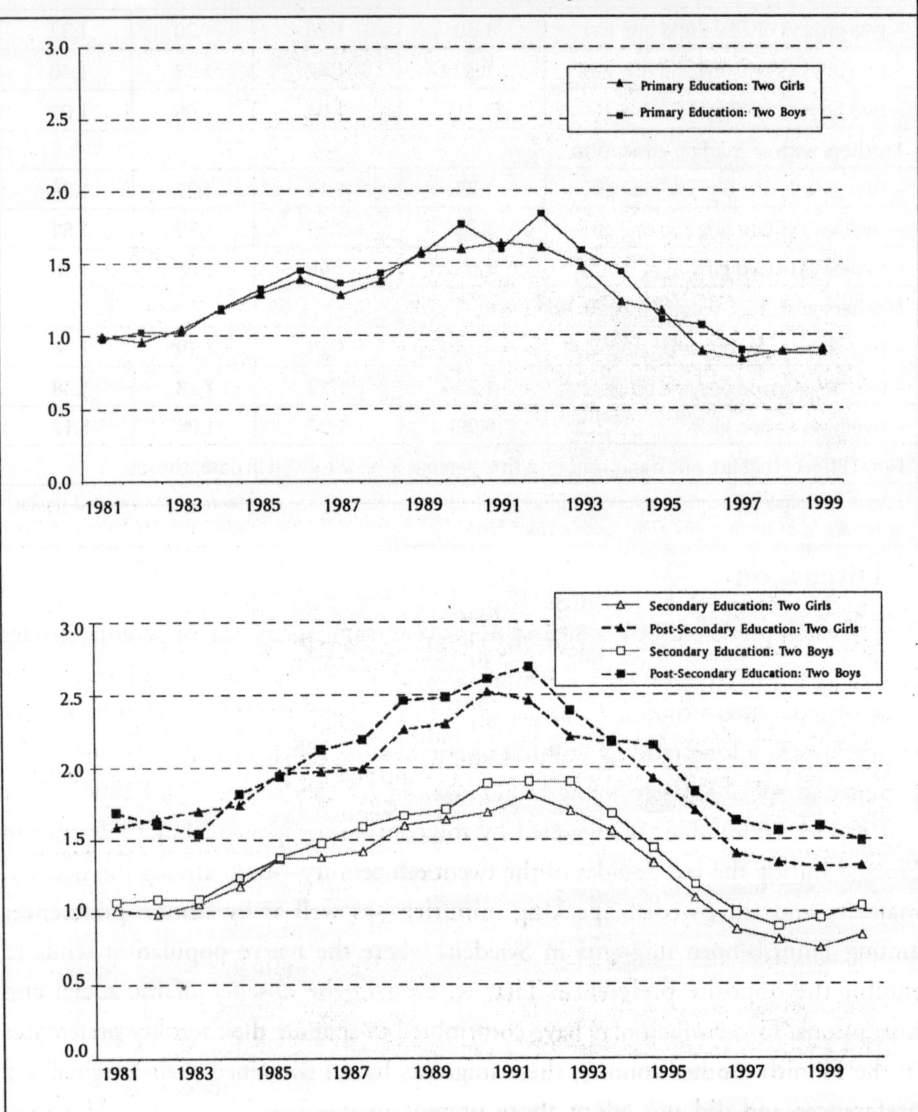

appear to be torn between, on the one hand, social influences they experienced in their family of origin (characterized by 'Finnish' preferences) and, on the other hand, social learning from Swedish peers (and/or native-born marriage partners): in this particular group we only detect a 'composition' preference in childbearing dynamics, but no indication for favouring a specific sex.

Apart from this, we find no evidence which supports diffusion theories of differential persistence and change in parents' sex preferences for children. For example, the Swedish girl preference, which fully emerged only in the 1980s, did not occur first in the Stockholm area to develop later in the less urban parts of Sweden, as one might have expected. Instead, our findings are rather in line with Sharlin's (1986: 258) conclusion from the observation of fertility decline during Europe's demographic transition, namely that behavioural change in the first place "occurs in discrete cultural areas (regions) and that urban-rural differentials are subsidiary differences within regions". Our findings suggest that at least in the contemporary Swedish-Finnish context national borders may be more efficient demarcations of such cultural areas than linguistic barriers are (cf. Watkins 1990). Finally, the absence of any evidence suggesting the diffusion of 'new' gender preferences from the more highly educated social strata into the general population of Sweden is consistent with other research on changes, in Swedish fertility dynamics by Andersson, Hoem and Duvander (2006), who could not detect any educational differentials in the timing and magnitude of responses to policy measures designed to foster more rapid continued childbearing in Sweden, during the 1980s (the so called 'speed premium').

To conclude, parental gender preferences and their impact on fertility decisions (as well as on other family events) may continue to be a demographically relevant topic in the twenty-first century. The reasons for the persistence and change in the demand for a specific sex or sex composition of children are still not well-understood. What, for example, was the triggering cause of the sudden and (geographically as well as socially) global emergence of girl preference in Sweden? Thus, further and ideally multidisciplinary research that helps to improve our understanding of this phenomenon is desirable. Nevertheless, we end with pointing out that the phenomena we have demonstrated still is fairly marginal, which we are able to detect with such precision merely because of the magnitude of our data and with apparent preferences for a child of a specific sex being much weaker than the desire for having a child of each sex. There are no signs that gender preferences for children in the Nordic countries are so strong that they have produced more drastic outcomes like sex-selective abortion (for related evidence from Germany and the US see Dahl *et al.*, 2003; 2006): a closer examination of our data (not shown) reveals that there is no tendency at all of any changes in the sex composition of children born by different demographic sub-groups, neither in Sweden nor in Finland.

6. Acknowledgements

Comments by Elizabeth Thomson, Laurent Toulemon, Gerda Neyer, Hill Kulu, and Livia Oláh are gratefully acknowledged. We would also like to thank the Statistical Central Bureaus of Finland and Sweden for providing us with the individual-level register data used in this analysis.

(Gunnar Anderson, Stockholm University, Stockholm. He can be reached at gunnar.andersson@sociology.su.se.

Karsten Hank, MEA – University of Mannheim & DIW Berlin. He can be reached at hank@mea.uni-mannheim.de.

Andres Vikat, United Nations Economic Commission for Europe, Geneva. He can be reached at andres.vikat@unece.org).

References

1. Andersson, G. (2004): Childbearing after migration: Fertility patterns of foreign-born women in Sweden. *International Migration Review,* 38 (2), 747-775.
2. Andersson, G., K. Scott (2005): Labour-market status and first-time parenthood: The experience of immigrant women in Sweden, 1981-97. *Population Studies,* 59 (1), 21-38.
3. Andersson, G., K. Scott (2007): Childbearing dynamics of couples in a universalistic welfare state: The role of labor-market status, country of origin, and gender. *Demographic Research,* forthcoming.
4. Andersson, G., G. Woldemicael (2001): Sex composition of children as a determinant of marriage disruption and marriage formation: Evidence from Swedish register data. *Journal of Population Research,* 18 (2), 143-153.

5. Andersson, G., K. Hank, M. Rønsen, A. Vikat (2006): Gendering family composition: Sex preferences for children and childbearing behavior in the Nordic countries. *Demography,* 43 (2), 255-267.

6. Andersson, G., J. Hoem, A.-Z. Duvander (2006): Social differentials in speed-premium effects in childbearing in Sweden. *Demographic Research,* 14 (4), 51-70, available at *http://www.demographic-research.org/Volumes/Vol14/4.*

7. Arnold, F. (1997): Gender preferences for children. *Demographic and Health Surveys Comparative Studies* No. 23. Calverton, MD: ORC Macro.

8. Axinn, W., S.T. Yabiku (2001): Social change, the social organization of families, and fertility limitation. *American Journal of Sociology,* 106 (5), 1219-1261.

9. Bianchi, S., M. Milkie, L. Sayer, J. Robinson (2000): Is anyone doing the housework? Trends in the gender division of household labor. *Social Forces,* 79 (1), 191-228.

10. Bongaarts, J. (2001): Fertility and reproductive preferences in post-transitional societies. *Population and Development Review,* 27, Supplement, 260-281.

11. Bongaarts, J., S. Watkins (1996): Social interactions and contemporary fertility transitions. *Population and Development Review,* 22 (4), 639-683.

12. Brockmann, H. (2001): Girls preferred? Changing patterns of sex preferences in the two German states. *European Sociological Review,* 17 (2), 189-202.

13. Brunborg, H. (1987): Gutt eller jente? Tidsskrift for den Norske Lægeforening, 107 (14), 1207-1209.

14. Bulatao, R. (1981): Values and disvalues of children in successive childbearing decisions. Demography, 18 (1), 1-25.

15. Cleland, J., J. Verrall, M. Vaessen (1983): Preferences for the sex of children and their influence on reproductive behaviour. World Fertility Surveys Comparative Studies No. 27. Voorburg, NL: ISI.

16. Dahl, E., M. Beutel, B. Brosig, K.-D. Hinsch (2003): Preconception sex selection for non-medical reasons: A representative survey from Germany. Human Reproduction, 18 (10), 2231-2234.

17. Dahl, E., R.S. Gupta, M. Beutel, Y. Stoebel-Richter, B. Brosig, H.-R. Tinneberg, T. Jain (2006): Preconception sex selection demand and preferences in the United States. *Fertility and Sterility,* 85 (2), 468-473.

18. Dahl, G.B., E. Moretti (2004): The demand for sons: Evidence from divorce, fertility, and shotgun marriage. *NBER Working Paper 10281,* Cambridge, MA.

19. Diekmann, A., K. Schmidheiny (2004): Do parents of girls have a higher risk of divorce? An eighteen-country study. *Journal of Marriage and Family*, 66 (3), 651-660.

20. Finnäs, F. (1997): Social integration, heterogeneity and divorce. The case of the Swedish-speaking population in Finland. *Acta Sociologica*, 40 (3), 263-277.

21. Finnäs, F. (2003): The Swedish-speaking population on the Finnish labour market. Year book of Population Research in Finland, 39, 19-29.

22. Gray, E.E., A. Evans (2005): Parity progression in Australia: What role does the sex of existing children play? *Australian Journal of Social Issues*, 40 (4), 505-520.

23. Hammel, E. (1990): A theory of culture for demography. *Population and Development Review*, 16 (3), 455-485.

24. Hammer, M., J. McFerran (1988): Preference for sex of child: A research update. Individual Psychology, 44 (4), 481-491.

25. Hank, K., H. Jürges (2007): Gender and the division of household labor in older couples: A European perspective. *Journal of Family Issues*, 28 (3), 399-421.

26. Hank, K., H.-P. Kohler (2000): Gender preferences for children in Europe: Empirical results from 17 FFS countries. Demographic Research, 2 (1), available at *http://www.demographic-research.org/Volumes/Vol2/1*.

27. Hank, K., H.-P. Kohler (2003): Sex preferences for children revisited: New evidence from Germany. *Population (English Edition)*, 58 (2), 133-144.

28. Hoffman, L., M.L. Hoffman (1973): The value of children to the parents. In: J. Fawcett (Ed.), Psychological Perspectives on Population, 19-76. New York: Basic Books.

29. Jacobsen, R., H. Møller and G. Engholm (1999): Fertility rates in Denmark in relation to the sexes of preceding children in the family. Human Reproduction, 14 (4), 1127-1130.

30. Kartovaara, L. (1999): Boy or girl? Does it matter and is it a coincidence or destiny? Paper presented at the European Population Conference 1999, The Hague, The Netherlands.

31. Lundberg, S. (2005): Sons, daughters, and parental behavior. *Oxford Review of Economic Policy*, 21 (3), 340-356.

32. Manski, C. (1995): Identification Problems in the Social Sciences. Cambridge, MA: Harvard University Press.

33. Marleau, J.D., J.-F. Saucier (2002): Preference for a first-born boy in western societies. *Journal of Biosocial Science*, 34 (1), 13-27.

34. Montgomery, M., J. Casterline (1996): Social learning, social influence, and new models of fertility. *Population and Development Review*, 22, Supplement, 151-175.

35. Morgan, S.P., D. Lye, G. Condran (1988): Sons, daughters and the risk of marital disruption. *American Journal of Sociology*, 94 (1), 110-129.

36. Pollard, M., S.P. Morgan (2002): Emerging parental gender indifference? Sex composition of children and the third birth. *American Sociological Review*, 67 (4), 600-613.

37. Raley, S., S. Bianchi (2006): Sons, daughters, and family processes: Does gender of children matter? Annual Review of Sociology, 32, 401-421. SCB (2003): Access to microdata in the Nordic countries. Report, Statistics Sweden, Stockholm. Available online at *http://www.micro2122.scb.se/Access_to_ microdata_in_the_Nordic_countries.pdf.*

38. Schullström, Y. (1996): Garçon ou fille? Les préférences pour le sexe des enfants dans les générations suédoises 1946-1975. *Population,* 51 (6), 1243-1245.

39. Seidl, C. (1995): The desire for a son is the father of many daughters. A sex ratio paradox. *Journal of Population Economics*, 8 (2), 185-203.

40. Sharlin, A. (1986): Urban-rural differences in fertility in Europe during the demographic transition. In: A. Coale, S. Watkins (Eds.), The Decline of Fertility in Europe, 234-260. Princeton: Princeton University Press.

41. Sloane, D., C.-F. Lee (1983): Sex of previous children and intentions for further births in the United States, 1965-1976. *Demography*, 20 (3), 353-367.

42. Stark, L., H.-P. Kohler (2002): The debate over low fertility in the popular press: A cross-national comparison, 1998-99. *Population Research and Policy Review,* 21 (6), 535-574.

43. Svanberg, I., H. Runblom (1988): Det mångkulturella Sverige. En handbok om etniska grupper och minoriteter. Stockholm: Gidluns bokförlag.

44. Thomson, E. (2001): Value of children. In: N.J. Smelser, P.B. Baltes (Eds.), *International Encyclopedia of the Social and Behavioral Sciences,* Vol. 8, 1725-1729. Amsterdam (and others): Elsevier.

45. Wallgren, A., B. Wallgren (2007): Register-based Statistics: Administrative Data for Statistical Purposes. Chichester: John Wiley and Sons.

46. Watkins, S. (1990): From local to national communities: The transformation of demographic regimes in Western Europe, 1870–1960. *Population and Development Review*, 16 (2), 241-272.

47. Westoff, C. (1999): Mass communications and fertility. In: R. Leete (Ed.), Dynamics of Values in Fertility Change, 237-251. Oxford, USA: Oxford University Press.

48. Wirth, L. (1938): Urbanism as a way of life. *American Journal of Sociology*, 44 (1), 1-24.

Index